# Conflict Resolution for Couples

## "Just the Tools" Edition

Paul R. Shaffer

authorHOUSE®

*AuthorHouse™ LLC*
*1663 Liberty Drive*
*Bloomington, IN 47403*
*www.authorhouse.com*
*Phone: 1-800-839-8640*

*Published by AuthorHouse    08/29/2014*

*ISBN: 978-1-4969-3615-8 (sc)*
*ISBN: 978-1-4969-3616-5 (hc)*
*ISBN: 978-1-4969-3614-1 (e)*

# Contents

# Dedication

There were three groups of people that struggled with the original "Conflict Resolution for Couples": 1) those men and women who were intimidated by the size of the book (almost 400 pages), 2) those people with ADD/ADHD who couldn't sustain their focus long enough to finish the reading, and 3) those who didn't share in my love of the over-use of bold type. This book is for you!

# Foreword

This being the "Just the Tools" edition of Conflict Resolution for Couples, you, the reader, may have some questions as to what differentiates this edition from its parent book (the last updated version being called "the Final Edit"). "The Final Edit" was an "everything plus the kitchen sink" effort on my part. It was 18 chapters long (twice the size of this book) and included six chapters on foundational aspects to relationships as well as three chapters on specialized populations (dating, affairs and considering separation). *This* edition is for those who wanted just the core concepts without all of the additional information. It consists of the conflict model, the ABC's (26 tools) of a "fair fight", and strategies for maintaining relationship change. It's "just the tools"; what you need to better move through any potential conflict, and make change last. Chapter 10 isn't from the conflict books, but I threw it in for free because 1) it was relevant to couple's conflict, and 2) ten is a better number to end a book on than nine. So, you're welcome!

◆ ◆ ◆

Experience has taught me that most people, myself included, do not have very good study skills. By this, I mean that most people, even though they can read and comprehend what they are reading, do not approach a book in a way that makes it likely that they will *retain* what has been read.

Most strategies learned in high school and college were *time-based* strategies. You learned what you needed for the test and then forgot about it. The focus was only on *short-term* retention. Keeping this in mind, I would like to suggest some strategies for approaching this book in a way that will make it likely to have a more meaningful and lasting impact on your life.

1. **For couples, one of the best ways to read this book is with the significant other.** I don't mean that you are both trying to read at the same time, but rather one person reads to the other. While this is not a necessity (or maybe even a possibility, depending on the situation), the benefits multiply immensely. When you read you typically make observations about the relationship in question or, sometimes, just about yourself that, in the moment, make a difference to you but, if the other person is not present, they often go unshared and then lost in time. As a result, it is a missed opportunity for feedback from and learning for the other.

Reading together becomes a team activity, something you are doing together for the sake of the relationship – visible evidence that you are willing to work on it, that you care. You will have a much more meaningful discussion if you are able to comment on things as they are being read, rather than after-the-fact.

If the relationship is currently hostile, it is likely that feedback on the relationship while reading together might be taken as an attack or a judgment and should probably be avoided. If the relationship is borderline hostile, but your partner is still open to reading along, then the suggestion would be to only make comments on the things you feel apply to you or the relationship, but *not* your partner. If reading together becomes a running critique of each other, then, unintentionally or not, you are sabotaging making this a potentially positive activity.

It *is* possible to apply the methods discussed in this book without the other ever having read it, but, for maximum effect, it is recommended that both parties do the reading.

2. **Take your time reading**. This is a very rushed civilization we live in. Everything is based around efficiency and saving time – which is somewhat ironic since we often become *less* efficient due to all the short-cuts. We lose quality in our search for quantity. Give yourself permission

to take the time to think through what you are reading. Don't let this be just another self-help book under your belt.

If you are truly wanting help with the quality of your relationship, it deserves the time spent in investigating solutions. Think of it in terms of someone panning for gold; if he goes too fast in his search he is likely to overlook what he is searching for. If you find yourself beginning to skim, you're going too fast.

Try to choose a peaceful moment to do your reading. If you're trying to squeeze it in in the middle of a hectic day, you will not be fully attending to what you're reading. You will be trying to shift mental gears to take in the content, but your background attention is going to be on watching the clock.

3. **Look for how what you are reading applies to your *own* life**. Many of you may think that you do this anyway – but often people will approach self-help reading as a method for learning about others without necessarily thinking about how it applies to them. Often couples reading this type of book will be looking for information about the significant other and overlooking opportunities for self-insight.

I continue to do therapy and support groups from time to time and it always amazes me how someone can be in a group for a while and eventually make the comment, "I just can't see how any of this relates to me." Learning by association is a skill. It involves looking for common threads, parallel meanings. They are always there if you look for them.

Emotional pain is a common experience that connects us all. Conflict in relationships is an everyday occurrence. While individual problems may be different, the strategies for solving them are useable across the board. It seems the majority of people who feel isolated and misunderstood often feel this way because they continue to focus on what makes them different rather than what makes them alike.

4. **Consider using a highlighter or underline when you read**. As you come across sections that strike a chord in you – whether because you are

in agreement or disagreement, or because it's a new insight or perspective that deserves further thought, or something that would be great to share with another – highlight them so you can come back to them later. In this way you are making the book an easy reference for later use and incorporating the parts that have the most significance for you.

If you have identified the personally relevant high points for yourself in this book, you are much more likely to come back and re-read it since you have such markers to show you where to go. If you fail to highlight or underline you are less likely to expend the energy later to go back and search the pages to try to find the memorable parts, and, as a result, lose those insights over time as your memory of what you read fades.

5. **Write down any insights you arrive at as you read**. Different than highlighting, if a statement sets off a series of thoughts for you that leads to some relevant conclusions or understandings, take the time to actually *write* your thoughts down in a notebook. You're not duplicating what's already written, but rather the line of thinking that the written words inspired.

Often I will ask clients to bring notebooks with them to sessions. This is because we will usually cover a lot of territory in a single session and there will probably be several relevant points or strategies identified. If the client is trying to retain it all without any source for hanging onto it other than by memory, much of it will often be lost.

Most people remember things based on what's called the "primacy" and "recency" effects. According to these "effects", you tend to remember the beginning and the end of an event (in this case, the beginning or ending of a chapter) and forget what happened in the middle. Logging insights is one way of retaining that elusive middle.

6. **Repetition is the key**. The only way to keep something active in your mind in order to make a conscious change in your life is to review it. Again and again. One frequently quoted statistic is that *if you want to make a behavior part of your lifestyle you must maintain that behavior consistently for at least 3 months for it to develop into a habit.*

Just because you intellectually learn a strategy for controlling your anger, it will do you no good if it's not actually applied. Think of it along the lines of the training that an athlete goes through – there is a repetition of exercises that train the body to do what it needs to do without thought. At first it is awkward, because the old thinking or behavior is stronger and more familiar. But, with repetition, we are carving a new pathway, one that initially requires intentional thought but, over time, can develop into a pattern of response that becomes second-nature.

**7. There are exceptions to every rule.** Just as I would caution you to look for how things relate to your situation, not how they differ, I would remind you that to everything in this book there is an exception. The reason I am making this point is because you need to read this book with discretion and creativity. The rules/tools listed here are *guidelines* with which you need to be flexible and fine-tune to fit the specifics of your own relationship. The basis for each of the rules is sound, but try not to approach them so rigidly that you are trying to fit a square peg into a round hole. (On the opposite end, there are some people who tend to look for exceptions in an attempt to *dismiss* the rule.) I recognize there is no way I can write a book that covers every aspect of conflict that might arise. So try to be flexible in your thinking, finding creative ways to use the tools described.

**8. Don't turn this into work.** Make it something positive. You are much more likely to retain what you are reading if you give it a chance and let yourself get into it. A new insight, a fresh way of looking at things, can be inspiring. Use the visual image of seeing yourself adding to your wealth of knowledge. You are continuing to grow by stretching yourself in new ways, entertaining new ideas or reviewing old ones that you may have forgotten.

◆ ◆ ◆

In writing a book, you have to make a decision up front how you are going to handle possessive and personal pronouns. Rather than "he/she" or "his/her" every few sentences I'm told it's better to choose one or the other. For the purposes of this book I'm choosing to use the masculine form (he/his/him) – not with the purpose of pointing the finger at men, or the likelihood that the majority of people reading this book will be women, but for consistency's sake. No offense to men OR women intended.

Enjoy the read!

# Chapter 1
# The Conflict Model

Conflict is inevitable in any relationship. Yet many people enter into relationships with the expectations that, if it's a good relationship, there should be *no* conflict. While this is a myth, when conflict inevitably does occur, people often end up incorrectly concluding that the relationship was a mistake.

People will deny, avoid, repress or ignore conflict in hopes that it will go away. But *a healthy relationship is often determined by how smoothly conflict can be negotiated, not ignored.* It is a skill that, even if not modeled by your caregivers while you were growing up, is learnable.

The fact that a couple actually has arguments is secondary compared to whether those arguments get resolved and how quickly the couple is able to recover and regroup after they occur.

There are natural dilemmas that exist with how you work through the relationship issues, especially when it comes to expressing your upset. If you squash your anger, pretend or act like it doesn't exist, you may have saved the day today, but it's going to eat away at you inside and either explode somewhere down the road or find other ways to get out. If you "let it fly", you risk saying things that you're probably going to regret, and maybe don't even mean, but, once said, can't be undone.

Paul R. Shaffer

Many people who have issues with anger do so because they feel, or the partner feels, that it's *not* okay to be angry. Because there is no "allowed" outlet provided for their upset, things build to a point where they finally explode. But one of the central concepts of conflict resolution is that *it's okay to express your upset, so long as you do it appropriately* – ideally, in a way that creates understanding, not further damage.

Controlling your temper is difficult because it goes *against* your natural instinct when you feel attacked or hurt. While your emotions are telling you to defend yourself by retaliating, or to run away, you're consciously choosing to ignore them, to stay put, to think things through and to work it out.

Learning how to manage your anger effectively is a skill, and, being a skill, it is learned – you aren't born with it. Sometimes you see it modeled for you by your parents, but other times you have to figure it out for yourself. It's learning how to control your nature until the control part itself becomes more natural for you.

Anger stems from hurt feelings which, in turn, stem from unmet or injured needs. Needs, by nature of their definition, are legitimate - they *have* to be met. *The problem is always in how we go about trying to meet them.*

In a romantic relationship, you *need* both emotional intimacy and security. So if you've got an issue with your partner, intimacy demands that you share that with him at some point or you will be moving towards *false* intimacy. Emotional *security*, in part, comes from knowing that you're safe in sharing your pain with your partner, that he can handle it.

Conflict resolution attempts to meet those underlying needs, but in a way that doesn't further complicate the issue.

◆　◆　◆

There is a natural progression as to how anger escalates over time, and what it becomes if it goes unchecked.

2

*Frustration* often comes from circumstances where somebody said or did something you perceived as negative, that you can't easily change, or is beyond your control.

*Anger* usually comes into play when frustration has gone unresolved over time, or if you feel you've been intentionally wronged.

*Resentment* usually sets in when your anger has no outlet or no resolution.

*Bitterness* results when chronic resentment has hardened your heart. Only a conscious act of true forgiveness can begin to reverse the process.

◆　◆　◆

People tend to operate in the extremes, so they often either stop too short or go too far in trying to resolve conflict.

Many are great at starting arguments, but never get far enough into the conversation to accomplish anything. They complain and retreat. If you're tempted to withdraw from an argument before you've been successful at explaining yourself, or have yet to reach a resolution on the issue, you probably need to face the discomfort of conflict and hang in there longer.

At the other end, if you've already said what you needed to say, have reached a workable solution, but now you're tempted to go back and underline your points, you probably need to stop where you are. Some can actually reach a solution, then take it too far and undo everything they've accomplished.

The extremes are always the easiest options to see. Our instincts also operate in extremes. When there is the presence of a threat our instincts are very basic: fight or flight. Attack or withdraw.

# Adult – Parent - Child

Eric Berne had a theoretical approach to relationships back in the 70's and 80's called *transactional analysis*. Berne said that there are three different types of communication "roles" that we assume in our relationships: the *Adult*, the *Parent* and the *Child*.

We naturally want to be treated as an Adult – with respect, equality, and fairness. Of all the roles, the Adult is the most balanced and mature. The ideal combination we're working towards in the relationship is Adult-Adult. Unfortunately, we often do not know how to *be* the Adult. We have all had experience with being children. And we've seen how parents behave – good and bad. But we may not have had good models of mature adults.

If you are in a relationship with someone who typically takes on the role of the Child, your tendency is going to be to assume the role of Parent to that Child in order to balance the situation.

Understand that just because a relationship is *balanced* does not mean that it is *healthy*. I can be married to a very hot-headed woman and, because I'm passive, things balance out – I absorb her temper blasts like a sponge so, ultimately, there's peace, even though I've become a doormat in the process. But that doesn't mean that I'm happy or that the relationship works.

The Parent-Child pattern is one of the most typical for adult couples. Whoever is acting as the Child will often do the very things that force the partner into being the Parent even though *neither* wants to have that role. The Child will do things that invite criticism, discipline and punishment. He may be oppositional to requests. He may throw tantrums and insults. He may attempt to manipulate, and not accept responsibility for his actions.

The difference between the Adult and the Parent in those situations is that the Adult does not get into a power struggle with the Child, while the Parent attempts to punish, judge or control. The Adult side-steps the temper tantrum and tries to get at the underlying unmet or injured needs. *The only person the Adult is concerned about maintaining control over is himself.*

It's not that the temper tantrum goes un-addressed. There is still accountability for inappropriate destructive actions, but the Adult is not attempting to parent the partner.

If you were the Adult and your partner was trying to be the Parent, you would focus on not reacting to the other's attempts at forcing compliance, but move beyond that and attempt to find a mutual compromise that addressed the needs of both.

The Parent and Child are easily pulled into a conflict, and quickly lose perspective. The Adult takes a step *back* from the conflict (though not out of the conversation) in order to keep perspective. He can discuss and confront, but he doesn't get sucked into it. His agenda is to get to the heart of the issue, not get distracted or pulled into a reactive cycle.

While there is a *tendency* for each of us to take on particular roles, often, in a relationship, and even within a conversation, the roles will switch back and forth.

We are not *always* striving to be the Adult. Sometimes it's okay to be the *positive* aspect of a Child, enjoying life and just being in the moment without having to consider responsibility. And sometimes it's okay to be the *positive* aspect of a Parent when that parent is a supportive one, attempting to educate, not control.

The concern would be when any one pattern became too rigid and did not shift to meet the needs of what was most appropriate in the current situation, or when the role of Adult was consistently absent during conflicts.

## Words of Power

Words can be used to hurt or to heal, but the weight that they possess is the emotional weight that we attach to them. The same word for one person can leave him completely unmoved, while, for the next person, it can set off all sorts of associated memories or feelings. Words are incredibly powerful and we need to learn when, and how, to use them.

Most of us are very skilled at knowing how to use words as weapons. We have been entrusted with the knowledge of each other's most private fears, failures, embarrassments and guilt. We have listened to our partners share these with us in confidence and felt closer to them for trusting us. Yet, when things "hit the fan" and tempers start to flair, how do we repay this most loved one for their past trust? Well, we prove our own untrustworthiness by using those most private things against them, violating the intimacy that was gained. And then, days after the smoke has settled, we have the nerve to express our frustration when we find they are hesitant to share with us again. We desire intimacy but so often abuse it once we've gained it.

By the time we are adults, we are typically very protective creatures who trust only in the smallest of degrees. We guard our secrets closely and to risk trusting another with them takes courage. For those who have already been hurt or betrayed in the past, it takes *incredible* courage.

Trust is the foundation of any relationship. If you don't have trust, then you don't have anything to build on. We *create* trust through the loving consistency in our words and actions. Thinking in these terms, it's easy to see how a lover can become an enemy - how love can shift to hate, if the trust is violated. If I am rejected by a stranger it means nothing because they meant little to me, and they really do not know who I am. If I am rejected or betrayed by my partner, it is the essence of who I am that is being judged, violated or discarded by the very person I trusted the most.

Even in your own life, apart from any relationship, the words you tell yourself shape the quality of your existence. You can impact the likelihood of having a great day or a bad one based on what words you tell yourself at its start. If you say to yourself, "Today's going to be a great day", then you've already chosen, at least to a degree, that today's going to be something to look forward to. If you get up and the first thing out of your mouth is "Oh, no, what's going to go wrong today?" you're already focused on finding the things that will confirm your fear of the day going badly.

People are often quite fragile when it comes to the opinions of others. Sometimes you can make or break someone else's day by a simple compliment or criticism. You can enforce your child's self-confidence or contribute to his fears based on what you verbally choose to recognize about him or his world.

Words can be so incredibly powerful and yet we often treat them with no regard. We gossip, we ramble on, we can talk at length about nothing at all.

When we attack, the hostile words flow with little editing involved, without filter. We may think that we're still in control, but we're actually somewhat out of control because our feelings are dictating what's coming out of our mouth, not our reason. Conflict resolution moves us back to re-focusing on self-control, and choosing our words thoughtfully, not recklessly. An emotionally out-of-control relationship becomes chaotic, so the beginning of restoring some degree of control is to restore a degree of structure to how we address each other.

## The Model

The key to the dilemma of what you do when you've been hurt is not *whether* you express that hurt, but *how* you express it. Much of the information we attempt to share in negative ways is still useful, it's just that we aren't delivering it in a way that's going to accomplish anything other than to escalate the situation.

What's going on with you when you're upset is more than just being angry. There are reasons *why* you're angry that need to be discussed.

You need to remember that your partner's personality and perceptions are different than your own. Even though you're both humans, you talk, think and feel things differently. You may have a lot in common, but you're not identical. You can't afford to assume that you're automatically understood, and you need to model what you want in return. If you want respect, show respect. If you want love, show love. But try to do it in a way that's meaningful to your partner. Even in the midst of conflict.

Why would you expect a verbal attack to draw you closer again, or withholding to create better understanding? A verbal attack pushes you further away from your partner. Withholding creates a gulf between the two of you. If what you really desire, past the anger, is restored closeness, then you need to forget the attack, or the withdrawal, and work towards a better way of being understood or seeking a resolution.

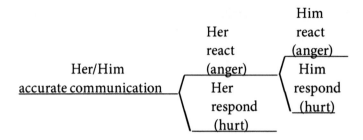

Above is a two-way model for resolving conflict where anger (or any strong emotion for that matter) is playing a part. It's a two-way model in that either party can intervene at any point to change the direction of the conversation – to escalate or de-escalate the situation. It can be used for dealing with either misunderstandings or when an actual issue is present.

Let's take it one piece at a time, since the diagram will make no sense until we start playing it out.

The straight line, labeled "accurate communication", is Tom and Tina having a conversation. At this point, for the most part, Tina's interpreting what Tom's saying accurately - they are hearing and understanding each other and generally getting along. (Realize that communication, with its nuances, tone and semantics, is never 100% accurate. It is more like a bumpy line than a straight one.)

Conversation, when it's done respectfully, is like a game of tennis. One person is talking at a time. When he's said his piece, then the ball is over in her court to add to what he said or move the conversation in a different direction. So, too, the conflict model is taking turns back and forth, moving things through to a resolution. Obviously, one of the difficulties for many arguments is that no one's taking turns – it becomes a struggle over who's going to dominate the conversation. But to regain control of the interaction, we must step back to taking turns (respectful communication).

Back to Tom and Tina. Let's say Tom makes a comment or does something that creates a bump in the up-until-then smooth road. The bump could be due to a misunderstanding or it could be an actual issue – we don't know yet. But whatever the case, for Tina, the impact was a hurtful one. Whether Tina realizes it or not, she now has five possible avenues to take:

- She can *let it go*, because she's able to truly forgive, or recognizes that it wasn't a big enough issue to actually discuss.
- She can *repress* it - act like nothing bothered her, when it did (which is different than letting it go because it *was* a big enough issue to discuss).
- She can *respond* – attempting to inform Tom that what he said hurt her.
- She can *react* - defensively (withdrawing) or offensively (attacking).
- She can give the *benefit of the doubt* - trying to clarify what he meant by what he said, rather than just assume that she took it correctly.

Sometimes we *do* need to let the little stuff go. We can't afford to make an issue out of everything. There does need to be room for grace in a relationship, without the expectation of perfection in our partner.

If she represses it, hopefully this isn't a pattern for her where she keeps sweeping things under the rug and it's starting to pile up. If so, sooner or later, things are going to start leaking out around the edges, usually building to an explosion.

Responding is a good choice, because it's attempting to educate your partner of something that you don't want them to repeat. However, it's still assuming that you took their intent correctly.

If she chooses to *withdraw,* it's different than repressing. To withdraw, you're still visibly angry but you're refusing to talk about it. Repression is where you swallow your upset and move on, *acting* like everything's okay when it's not.

The problem with both repressing and withdrawing, if they are never addressed further down the road, is that, if this is actually a misunderstanding, we're walking away with an incorrect assumption of what was meant, and never taking the time to find out if we understood correctly. If this is our pattern, we may have formed some extreme misconceptions of our partner over the years by doing so. Ideally, we should still brave a brief discussion to test the accuracy of our interpretation before we decide to address it or let it go.

If she reacts by attacking, the fight is usually on.

If she gives the benefit of the doubt, she recognizes that there still remains the possibility that she mis-interpreted what was said or done, and her first effort needs to be finding out if she took things correctly.

For the purposes of this model, we're going to focus on *reacting, responding* and *benefit of the doubt*.

**Scenario #1. Everybody Loses (Reacting).**

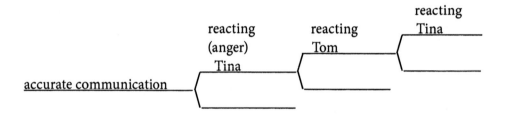

Let's start with the "worst-case scenario". This is the pattern that *reactive couples* take.

Tina is upset and so she *reacts*. Reacting (going with instinct) leaves us with the two choices of attacking or withdrawing (while still angry). In this particular situation, Tina is going to choose to attack.

Referring to the model, the communication has split between her anger (the top line) and her hurt (the bottom line). She's got a choice, whether she realizes it or not, of which way to go.

Between when Tom made his remark and before Tina first speaks in reaction, she has a split-second conversation in her head about what Tom meant by what he said. She *assumes* a hurtful meaning which leads to her reaction.

By going with her anger, she is *unintentionally* moving the conversation further away from the underlying hurt which is at the root of her upset. If she reacts by attacking, she *thinks* she's expressing her hurt, but it's only the anger that's coming out, diverting her partner from the reason *why* she's angry. While Tina probably feels that she *is* addressing the issue, she's actually turning Tom's focus to her unwarranted attack. (I say "unwarranted" because, in this situation, Tina misinterpreted Tom's actions.)

◆　◆　◆

Now it's Tom's turn to choose between reacting to Tina's reaction or responding in a way that gets at her underlying hurt. Since Tina *did* react, Tom will most likely be focused on the unfairness of her reaction, rather than thinking about *why* she is reacting this way. If it's obvious to Tom that she just misinterpreted what he said or did, then he knows that she just assumed the worst about his intentions rather than giving him the benefit of the doubt. And not only did she assume the worst, but she's now inappropriately attacking him rather than respectfully addressing him with her upset.

He has the same choice that Tina had, to react or respond, but because he's now over-focusing on her negative behavior, rather than thinking about his own, he will predictably react in turn.

With each interchange, the emotion escalates, moving the couple further and further away from the core of the issue and more and more into the side-issues brought up by the reactions.

There's a paradox here in that while each is engaged in a verbal control struggle, *each is actively giving up his control by waiting for the other partner to do the right thing first.* Someone needs to take back control of his own part.

◆　◆　◆

After Tom's reaction to Tina's reaction, the ball is now back in Tina's court. Even though it was Tina who initially verbally attacked Tom, she is still unrealistically expecting a vulnerable, sincere, mature response from him that addresses her hurt and not her anger. She's not thinking about how her reaction just made that very unlikely to occur. So when Tom reacts, rather than seeing what she did that led to his reaction, Tina now feels even more justified to continue to react because Tom's essentially confirming for her, by his negative behavior, that her initial negative assumption was correct.

So Tina continues to keep the reactive cycle going even though it was actually she who started this fight, not Tom, by failing to question her negative assumption and just reacting.

The situation continues to escalate until someone either loses all control, shuts down or storms off. What started out as a simple conversation and a possible misunderstanding quickly escalated into a major incident simply because no one knew how to stop the process.

For reactive couples, 60 to 70 percent of their arguments are potentially due to misunderstandings because they don't take the time to successfully correct the initial assumptions. And even if those misunderstandings *are* cleared up over the course of the argument, it's only after much additional damage has been done.

**Scenario #2. Tom comes through (Responding).**

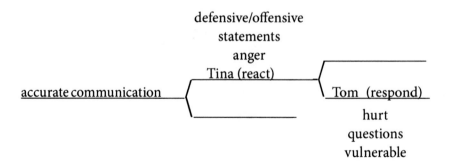

Okay, now let's take the same situation and give Tom some better tools to work with. Tom makes a comment. Tina misunderstands or takes issue with what was said and, once again, reacts. (Don't worry, she'll do better later.)

This time, however, Tom's got it together and does the smart thing. Tina's angry response is his cue that something's gone amiss. He knows immediately that, instead of reacting to Tina's hostility, which is masking or leading him away from what's actually going on, he needs to get to the bottom of it - the hurt that's underneath. He knows that even though her present grievance may be unfounded, the underlying need that's been hurt is legitimate.

So how does he get to the hurt?

He simply, sincerely, *responds* with a question. He *asks*.

Tom says something profound like, "What's got you so upset? What did you hear me say?"

Now if his tone is concerned, or at least neutral, and he really sounds like he's interested in wanting to know, a number of things will be accomplished all at once.

- There is a reason that Tom intervenes with a question rather than a statement. *A question does not attempt to define reality for your partner; it is asking him to define his reality for you.* If your partner has just reacted, which usually is because he has assumed an attack or insensitivity on your part, a *sincere* question indicates that you're not trying to invalidate his experience. It doesn't invalidate the reaction, and yet it doesn't feed into it either. Most *reactions* are expressed through statements, telling the partner what he needs to do or stop doing, or what kind of person he is for having done it. And if questions are asked, often they are done in a hostile tone that doesn't invite vulnerability. "I can't believe you could be so insensitive." "You need to shut up." "That's a lie." "What's your problem?"

- Statements are often perceived as attempts to control the situation. "You need to calm down," is the Parent talking to the Child. Your partner may be acting like a Child, but it's not your job to be the Parent. You are trying to help him step back into an Adult role. "What did you hear me say?" or "How did you interpret what I said?"

is a pretty smart thing for Tom to ask. It's automatically pointing out that what Tina heard might not have been what Tom meant, leading Tina to doubt her assumption. Other options might be "What did you think I meant by that?" or "Why was that hurtful to you?"

- By not giving Tina something else to react to, Tom is not adding any more fuel to the fire. He is stopping the progression up the conflict ladder and he is also removing himself from the pattern of conflict that they may have had in the past.

- By not reacting, Tom is actually holding up a mirror to Tina. Hers is the only raised voice. Hers are the only hostile words. If Tom is successful in keeping his cool and not buying into her aggression, sooner or later Tina's going to become self-aware that she's the only one acting rashly here.

- The most important reason for using questions is because *people can't fully think and feel at the same time* – it involves two different areas of the brain. If I give you a math problem when you're upset you're going to do one of two things: solve the problem because anger took a back-seat, or not be able to solve the problem because your feelings got in the way of thinking it through. One of the two will dominate. The best way to de-escalate hurt feelings is to make that transition from feelings (emotional logic) to thought (rational logic). So, if you ask a question, especially one that requires some self-analysis, you're helping your partner move past reacting, and on to *thinking* about what's going on – Why did that actually hurt? You're still asking about feelings, true, but you're putting it on an objective level. You're helping your partner find some emotional distance from the problem in order to resolve the problem; and you're de-escalating the tension at the same time.

If this was a misunderstanding and Tom is now able to redirect Tina to her incorrect interpretation, and correct it, the conversation only strayed but slightly before it was brought back on track, saving the couple from a potentially very ugly interaction.

Tom's response was a *controlled* reaction. He might have still been upset about how Tina reacted, but he managed his own emotions and kept the conversation focused in a healthy direction.

**Scenario #3. Tina does Good (Benefit of the Doubt).**

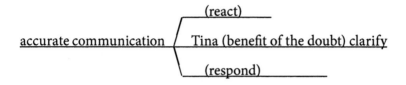

Alright, this last scenario is where Tina nips it in the bud.

Tom makes his statement that sets something off in Tina. Tina finds the statement insulting for whatever reason, but, instead of reacting, Tina does the most difficult thing. She gives Tom *the benefit of the doubt*. She doesn't automatically *assume* that he's trying to hurt her. She tries first to find out if what she heard was accurate. She recognizes the possibility of her own error in interpreting.

Benefit of the doubt recognizes that what my partner does or says, even if they do it three days in a row, can be for a totally different reason each day. More than that, in any particular instance, why we do what we do often is not for just one reason but several reasons that come together in that single moment. It recognizes our complexity, rather than over-simplifying our behavior into just a single negative motivator.

Level-headed Tina knows that Tom loves her and wouldn't intentionally do something to cause her pain. (Now if Tom *does* have a past pattern of doing things to intentionally hurt her, with words or deeds, then it's going to be much more difficult for Tina to give the benefit of the doubt, but it doesn't change the fact that it's still necessary if they want to move things ahead in a healthy direction.)

So Tina steps in with "Tom, I'm not sure what you meant by that. What I *thought* you meant was (fill in the blank). Is that accurate?"

She just indicated her possible confusion (a vulnerable stance, not a defensive one), told him her interpretation of what she heard him say, and then asked for confirmation.

Tom may say, "No, that's not what I meant at all" and explain himself and Tina finds out it was just a misunderstanding. And no one has to walk out the door, or manage their blood pressure. All that energy saved because of one simple step.

Note that I didn't even suggest that Tina *respond* to Tom. To respond would be attempting to educate Tom about how he'd hurt her, but Tina didn't know yet whether she had a right to be hurt. She first needed to *clarify* Tom's meaning before she would have an idea of where to go from there.

## Conspiracy Theories

When the benefit of the doubt goes away, it's often replaced with *conspiracy theories.* Conspiracy theories are the pieces that we put together over time that explain our partner's behavior to us. They are usually based on actual experience, but it still leaves it up to us to make sense of those experiences. Sometimes those theories can be correct, but other times they are wildly inaccurate and only serve to stand in the way of the relationship progressing. Often, they feed our own insecurities, fears or resentments.

The problem with conspiracy theories is that, once they've crystallized, they don't allow for contradictory information. Everything that happens now feeds the theory. If the theory is "He doesn't love me anymore," her attention is only going to be focused on those continuing experiences that fit the theory. And now each of those little experiences is going to provoke a larger reaction from her because they've come to mean something very big.

Even when he behaves in a way that *doesn't* fit her theory, this behavior will tend to be ignored, minimized or distorted by her. So if he does something that's actually loving, her internal interpretation might still be,

"He's just doing that because he feels guilty." So the possible negatives get most of her focus and the positives no longer carry any weight.

*His* experience of this is a "damned if I do, damned if I don't." No matter what he does, it's going to be the wrong thing for her because she's looking for the negative in all of it. He may not even be aware of her underlying theory. He just knows that no matter what he says or does, it doesn't seem to make a difference, or she doesn't seem to believe him.

When a theory exists, it needs both parties involved to dismantle it.

1.  The benefit of the doubt has to be re-embraced, where we start to allow for explanations other than the one that's easiest for us to reach for.

2.  The person with the theory has to recognize her own theory and stop feeding it, since she will tend to think on it and distress herself with it even when he's not there to fuel it.

3.  The person who helped create the theory, has to know what he's doing that's keeping it alive. He needs to either change what he's doing that contributes to it, or do a better job of explaining himself if her interpretation is inaccurate.

The harder theories to dismantle are the ones that were there before the relationship started. ("Women can't be trusted." "Men are only in it for one thing.") These are often underlying beliefs that have formed from previous relationships or what we witnessed in our own homes growing up - maybe even our parent's conspiracy theories that have been passed on to us. The problem with these unhealthy beliefs is that, even with rational evidence to the contrary, since they're beyond reason, they persist and can hold us back from drawing closer.

When it comes to irrational feelings or unhealthy beliefs, *the primary way to weaken them is to choose to live in a way that challenges their truth.* Otherwise, the more I cater to negative feelings, the more I increase the likelihood of a negative outcome. If I become lost in my fear that my partner is going to leave me, the more I will typically do things that push him away and make my abandonment likely. The more I feed my fears, acting like they're true, the stronger a hold they have over me.[1]

At the same time, the more I choose to *act* the part of a loving partner, and *think* loving thoughts, the more likely I will be able to reconnect myself to loving feelings towards him, and incite a loving reaction in him. People often get the sequence wrong. Their feelings dictate their behavior. But for the emotionally disciplined, they have learned to guide their emotions by how they choose to act and what thoughts they choose to entertain.

I don't mean to promote deluding yourself about who your partner is if abuse, chronic deceit, or an affair has occurred. In those cases, you need evidence of change, or evidence of the truth, more than naively just trusting. Here I'm referring to those situations where our perception has become distorted and now it's standing in the way of the relationship working because the benefit of the doubt no longer exists.

## The Physiology of Anger

When I referred to how we can't fully think (rational logic) and feel (emotional logic) at the same time, there's an important biological piece to better understanding this.

Hang in there with me for a minute, while I get a little scientific. The limbic system, at the base of your brain, is the first part of the brain to develop. It's often referred to as the "old brain", and is where our *instincts* and *primitive emotions* reside.

The neo-cortex, or "new brain", is the top layer of the brain and the last part of your brain to develop – usually maturing somewhere between ages 17 to 24. It's where your *higher reasoning* abilities are located.

When our brain experiences an event, often the information gets filtered through the limbic system first. If the information is benign or familiar, it continues on to be processed by other parts of the brain. If the information is stimulating (in a positive or negative way), it sets off an excitatory

---

[1]    I'll spend more time talking about this in Chapter 8.

response, activating our base emotions - which is why our initial reaction to surprises is instinctive.

At the point the limbic system gets over-stimulated, due to a perceived threat, the information process gets halted, because our primitive brain has gone into "survival mode". This is unfortunate, because what you want to be able to do most in a crisis is think, but that's usually the hardest thing to do in those moments. For the information to be able to go on to the neo-cortex where it can be properly processed (thought through), the alert level has to be lowered.

So when an argument begins and reactions start to occur, limbic systems activating, each continued reaction keeps the "old brain" over-stimulated to the point that nobody's actually thinking anymore, just emotionally reacting. In order for rational thinking to prevail, somebody has to stop adding fuel to the fire.

This is why it's so important in heated conversations to buy enough time that each of us can actually start thinking things through. *If we just continue to give each other more things to react to, the necessary parts of our brain never get involved.*

Again, that's why questions are so important in helping us engage on a rational level - they help us start to think.

It *is* possible to train our brains to be less reactive. The brain often acts like a muscle in that the parts we exercise the most result in the best developed neural pathways. It is much easier for someone who regularly exercises the rational part of his brain to manage his feelings. But just because someone may be more feeling-based, doesn't mean that he can never learn emotional control.

## When Questions Don't Work (Healthy Exits)

There are times during an argument when questions, even good questions, backfire. At the point that someone is over-whelmed emotionally, to try to engage him in thinking things through can actually agitate his frustration rather than de-escalate it. It's like going full-out in fifth gear and then trying to shift into reverse. It's too much of a transition for the brain to make.

While it doesn't mean you should be afraid to try questions, it does mean that when you find it's heating things up rather than cooling things down, that's your cue to shut down the conversation and re-approach it once things have had time to settle.

The term that I use for ending an argument that is becoming out of control, is taking a "*healthy exit*".

There are two rules for taking healthy exits:

## Rule #1. Either of you retains the right to end a heated conversation.

Of course, there are good ways and bad ways of leaving a conversation. Throwing up your hands and walking off is not a good way. Throwing out a final insult and then trying to shut the conversation down is also not a good idea. Hanging up on your partner is not the best of choices.

Respectful communication requires stepping back and saying something like, "I need for us to walk away from this for the moment. I'm feeling like things are too heated and I might say something that I don't really mean". You're taking responsibility for your behavior by doing this, and stopping things before bridges get burned.

If you said, "I'm stepping out because you're obviously losing it," or, "I'm taking a walk because you're saying things you're gonna regret", it could incite another reaction. But you could say, "This is getting too intense for me. I need to step away from this and give things time to cool down." Or, simply, "I need to take a time-out."

The couple needs to decide for themselves what appropriate exit lines to use that have the highest odds for success.

The unspoken part of this first rule is that *whoever is asking to end the argument is given the room to withdraw.* Many couples who've turned things into a control struggle will attempt to force the partner back into the conversation by following him through the house or continuing to try to re-engage him in the argument. If your partner's already said he can't continue, then you need to respect that. By continuing to push things when he's already said he's at his limit, you're asking for a reaction.

If what you want at that point is to still work things out, you need to accept that you're not going to make any further progress by trying to push.

## Rule #2. Whoever is leaving the conversation agrees to take responsibility for bringing the issue back.

Often the reason why one partner is panicked about letting the other escape the argument is that there has been a pattern of avoidance in the past. Issues are approached and the partner continues to take an escape route rather than work things through.

One way of getting around this dilemma is him being responsible for bringing the issue back to his partner rather than making her feeling obligated to have to bring it up again. If she knows that he will treat the issue with respect and assume responsibility to bring it back, he's teaching her that she doesn't have to try to control things.

Each side needs to be respectfully handling his part – letting the partner go and the partner coming back on his own.

Often you will need to attach a time-frame to how much time the two of you will take to calm down, rather than to just leave it hanging. This is especially true if there's a deadline pending for a decision. It can become a control issue if the withdrawing partner just takes his merry time re-approaching, and doesn't give any indication of how long he needs to take.

Ideally, couples need to try to re-approach within 24 hours rather than letting things linger for days at a time. It depends on how big the issue is and how much thought is required. At the point the couple re-approaches, it should be with some better ideas about how to move through the issue this time.

◆　◆　◆

Another dilemma concerning questions is that sometimes your partner, in that moment, doesn't know *why* he is upset, and trying to get at it past the point that he is able to think it through presents a new problem. If your partner doesn't know why he is upset, you don't have to make a project of digging it out. You can simply agree to give him time to figure it out.

If you know your partner well, you can still help soothe things in the meantime by falling back to whatever his "love language"[2] is: holding him, spending some time with him, supporting him with words, etc.

──────────────────

The conflict examples I gave are simplified ones in order to underline the steps. The reality is that arguments are typically not consistently either reacting or responding, but a combination of both. Things may start out well (responding) and then devolve into reacting, or things may start out with a poor delivery and then get corrected. Or it may go back and forth between the two as the conversation proceeds, each partner briefly recovering and trying to do the right thing only to get pulled back in again and the fight once more deteriorates. In other words, arguments are often not a step-by-step progression but a competitive mess. I tend to think of it as a couple trying to dance but who keep stepping on each other's toes. The faster you go with these conversations, the harder it's going to be to catch the mistakes, and get any better at it.

Ultimately, we are trying to learn to be more consistent with doing the things that actually work.

◆　◆　◆

──────

[2]　See Gary Chapman's "The Five Love Languages".

22

Almost anyone can handle things when they are going relatively well. What distinguishes our character is how we handle things when they're *not* going well. Do we attack, blame, run? Or do we face the test of character, show some self-discipline, and work it through.

Healthy love thinks of the good of the relationship, the future well-being of *both* people involved. Unhealthy love tends to be focused on self, and doing what feels good in the moment (yelling, attacking, etc.) at the cost of the relationship's future.[3]

You or your partner may learn to ignore the temper tantrums, or not respond to the hurtful things that are said. That may be how the relationship has survived. But you would be mistaken to assume that that means that everything's okay. Because one person has learned to "take it" does not mean that they will be able to, or even should, continue to "take it" over time. It wears on a person.

Other relationships survive by remaining superficial. They avoid the deeper topics that set off issues, having learned not to rock the boat. But usually this is at the cost of any deeper emotional intimacy.

The secondary damage that is done when we have not learned how to resolve our conflicts peaceably is reflected in our children, the habits that they are going to imitate. If we don't care enough about ourselves or our partner to learn how to temper our angry words, then perhaps we care enough about our kids to teach them better ways. It all starts with us.

## Summary Points:

1.  It's important to be able to express anger and frustrations. The key is doing it in a way that you are *heard*, not feared or resented.

2.  Conflict resolution does not come naturally. To remain vulnerable in the face of a perceived attack goes against instinct.

---

[3]    Scott Peck's "The Road Less Traveled."

3.  People often stop short or go too far in an argument. The goal is to go far enough to reach a resolution and no further.

4.  Communication is never 100% accurate.

5.  If something your partner says or does upsets you, make sure you truly understand what's going on before you respond to it. Practice giving *the benefit of the doubt.*

6.  Don't get distracted by the surface emotion of anger. Try to get at what's going on underneath – the hurt that's causing it.

7.  You can defuse a situation by introducing reason. Ask *questions*; don't make statements. Calm the emotion by helping your partner to think, not giving him more to react to.

8.  It's important to respect each other's need to end the conversation if things have gotten too heated with a promise (and even committing to a time) to return to the problem when both are less upset – taking a *healthy exit.*

## Discussion Questions:

1.  **Why is it so hard to extend the benefit of the doubt?** What is the damage done if the benefit of the doubt no longer exists? How do you restore the benefit of the doubt?

2.  **Which path do you tend to take when issues come up – responding or reacting?** If reacting, aside from your partner, what prevents you from changing that pattern? How much of how you approach an issue depends on your partner's state of mind rather than yours?

3.  **What percentage of your arguments do you think are actually based on misunderstandings?** Do you understand that if you aren't addressing the initial upset, there may be a whole lot of things that were initially misunderstandings that become issues because they were never clarified?

4. **What prevents you from remaining vulnerable to your partner when you discuss an issue?** What can you do to remove those obstacles?

5. **Are you able to stop an argument before it "burns the house down"?** What makes it so difficult to step out of a conflict when it gets that heated? How do you attempt healthy exits?

# Chapter 2
# When an Issue Exists

So let's say that when Tina clarifies things with Tom she finds out that she took things correctly; it *wasn't* a misunderstanding. So now she has an actual issue she needs to discuss with Tom. Where does she go from there?

The guidelines for the conflict model still continue to apply. Tina still needs to continue to speak from her hurt and not her anger - attempting to respond rather than react - exploring things with questions, each giving the benefit of the doubt as they go.

Let me clarify for a moment what I mean when I say "speaking from the hurt" when you respond. *In relationships, we typically don't get angry because we're angry, we're angry because we've been hurt.* The hurt is the truer emotion. Usually, the bottom line for *why* we're hurt is because we care and thought that our partners cared about us too. If we're able to bring our injured heart into the discussion early on, it's such a vulnerable move that it usually promotes a vulnerable response from our partners – it invites them in, rather than pushes them away. For example, "Do you understand that when you say that, it's hurtful to me? It comes off like you don't care about my feelings."

Rather than being a victim to reactions, we need to handle them wisely. In other words, because my partner is taking all of his cues from me as to whether he's going to be reasonable or get upset, I need to handle the control he's unintentionally giving me in a responsible way. By remaining open and focused, I'm more likely to get the same in return.

The ideal progression for conflict resolution, when it involves a deeper issue, looks like this:

1. **Identification**
2. **Validation**
3. **Explanation**
4. **Resolution**

## Step 1. Identify the Issue

By attempting a discussion, Tina is continuing to go *against* her instinct by trying to work things out rather than stepping back to reacting. *Often it's in times of emotional pain that we have our greatest opportunities to connect on a deeper level with our partners by showing them that we are safe to talk to, that we can be there for them even if their issue is with us, that we won't run away, that we won't react with an attack or a deflection.*

Sticking with responding, Tina's going to attempt to educate Tom about why what he said hurt. It may not change his opinion about what he said, but, now, knowing that it is an issue for Tina, at the least, he will probably be more careful next time. And it may not even be an issue with the core of *what* he was saying, just with *how* he said it, so hopefully he will be left with a better course to take in the future.

Let's say that Tom made a decision without consulting Tina; maybe it involved their mutual finances, and he's just now informed her about it. Tina might choose to say something like this:

"Tom, I have a real problem with what you did. To me, it's saying that you don't care about my opinion or what also belongs to me. I need to feel involved when you make decisions about how our money is spent."

Okay, you may not be able to see yourself talking like that, but don't get hung up on my words; pay attention to what's being said. Apply your *own* words to the situation. Tina's accomplished a number of things by the statements she just made.

- She's getting across that she isn't feeling valued and she wants to feel involved (she's addressed the injured needs).
- She's letting him know that that's not OK with her.
- She isn't passing judgment on him for doing it ("You're so insensitive.")
- She's also gone the extra mile by suggesting a future *solution* – to involve her in the decision process if it involves their mutual income.

She managed to get across that Tom hurt her and why (*identify*), and what he could do to avoid hurting her again in that way (*resolve*). She covered her bases and didn't even have to start throwing things. Now, obviously, the conversation doesn't stop there. The ball is back in Tom's court. But Tina's done a great job in a very short time of getting to the core of the problem.

Another option, consistent with the conflict model, Tina could have turned her statement into a question, "Tom, do you understand why I would have a problem with what you did?" If he gets it, then an explanation isn't even necessary.

◆　◆　◆

The dilemma with "identifying the issue" usually occurs when our *delivery* is a poor one. If we just bring up issues when we're upset we typically haven't thought it through, so while we may just be intending to vent, how it comes across is an attack.

Bringing up issues is often our attempt to hold our partners accountable, but many times our delivery comes across as a judgment, an ultimatum, or a rejection, rather than necessary information.

A useful tool is, when you're not in the middle of an argument, asking your partner for feedback on the ways that are best for you to raise issues with him, in the same way that he needs to know how best to approach you.

## Step 2. Validate the Issue

The next part of this, Tom's part, is, in my opinion, the number one "hang-up" for most couples in resolving conflict. Most couples, if they are having a very difficult time in getting to the *resolution* stage, are usually stuck in the *explaining* stage. And they get stuck because they keep skipping *validation.*

If Tom goes right into explaining why he did what he did, then what he's doing unintentionally is *invalidating* Tina's reaction. She's saying she's hurt and he's basically saying "You shouldn't be." He's still attempting to address it as if there's a misunderstanding, but Tina already knows what happened and she's not looking for further explanation, *at least not yet.* She's looking for her hurt to be *acknowledged*, and Tom's attempting to dismiss it. He isn't doing this to be cruel, it's just that an explanation is the most natural path to take.

By not involving her financially, it gave a hurtful message. He needs to give recognition for her pain ("I understand why you feel hurt, and I'm sorry, I didn't mean to hurt you."), explore it further if he or she feels they need more details, and move on to agreeing on a solution ("In the future, I'll consult you before I do anything.").

◆　◆　◆

Let me briefly describe different options for validation.

Sometimes simply *listening* can be validating. By showing respect for our partners and not trying to rush them through their issues, not jumping in with our opinion before they've had a chance to finish, or not trying to too quickly just solve it for them, we're giving them the attention they desire. Further, the more we take the time to explore their issues to better convey our desire to understand them, the more they'll feel heard.

The visual I attach to this is that of a Rubik's cube. When your partner approaches you with an issue, he basically just dropped a Rubik's cube in your lap, and he needs you to take a look at it, turn it a couple of different ways first to be sure you're actually understanding what this particular cube is about, *even if you think you already get it.*

Beyond listening, there's *acknowledging.* Acknowledgement is *not* agreement; it is simply recognizing your partner's perspective. There's almost always a certain logic, at least a partial truth, to his thinking. You need to take the time to understand how he's connecting the dots. True, there may be more dots involved that he's not considering, but it usually makes sense that he's coming to the conclusion that he is with only the dots that are in his line of sight. We need to start with the dots he's focused on, even if we don't agree with what he's concluding from them. ("If that's how you're putting it together, I can understand why you'd feel that way.")

Beyond acknowledgement, there's *apologizing.* That's not to say that you would apologize for something you didn't do. Let's say your partner thinks you intentionally did something to hurt him. You wouldn't apologize for intentionally hurting him if it was actually unintentional. But you *could* still apologize for the pain it caused, unintentional as it was.

For the record, "I'm sorry you took it that way," is not an actual apology. You're saying you're sorry for your partner's mistake, but an apology is at least partial ownership of what *you* did. "I'm sorry it came across like that, that wasn't my intent."

Beyond apologizing, there's *ownership.* Ownership is simply accepting fault or blame. If he was right and you screwed up, the easiest path to resolution is simple ownership of the wrong. "You're right, I shouldn't have done that."

At the same time, *ownership loses its value if we've overly applied it in the past, yet nothing has changed.* More than ownership at that point, we need to talk about what actual strategies or solutions we're willing to commit to, and be held accountable for.

◆　◆　◆

Some people will sabotage their own efforts to be validated. For instance, someone is angry to the point that he says some very hurtful things to his partner, but then acts surprised and becomes more upset because his pain is not being validated. However, *by expressing his anger inappropriately he just made sure validation was not going to occur.*

When I promote validating your partner's hurt, I'm not suggesting you try to validate the inappropriate angry behavior. You can't verbally slap somebody in the face and then complain that they're not trying to be affectionate or vulnerable. It would be like knocking the legs out from under someone and then criticizing him for not standing.

◆　◆　◆

If you feel like you can't validate what your partner is asking you to, find something else in what he's saying that you can.

If he's seeking validation for how he's been managing his money ("I've been doing well with my money this past month, yet you haven't said a thing."), yet you immediately think of all the times this past month that that didn't prove to be true. You could *in*validate his issue ("How can I say it, if it isn't true?"), or you could choose to focus on those times in the past month where he *did* succeed. ("Yes, there's been times this month where you did what you said you were going to do, and I appreciate those efforts.")

Some people will be hesitant with this because it's only a partial truth, and not completely accurate. But this is failing to recognize that you sometimes need to separate validation from a more complete explanation in the same way that you need to separate a compliment from a criticism. Better to say, "Honey, you look great in that dress," and leave it there, than to add, "but I really don't like those shoes." If you combine the two, the compliment never gets heard. That doesn't mean you ignore accountability for what he said he was going to do, but you are careful not to invalidate the small successes along the way. Those successes, and the positive reinforcement that he gets from you for it, is what motivates him to continue to improve in his consistency.

There is such a thing as *over-listening*, where you're paying too much attention to the details and accuracy of what your partner is saying, and, as a result, always in disagreement with him. *Paying attention to the content of what is being said is more important than the details of how it's said.*

For me, it's important to be accurate with my words because I have a strong need to be understood clearly. So I put a lot of energy into trying to be precise, but I recognize that the majority of the world is somewhat sloppy with their wording - vague, over-generalizing, distorted, etc. If I corrected a couple in couple's counseling for every time their wording was poor, we would never get through the session. And often that's what makes it difficult for the couple to progress in a conversation is because they're too closely monitoring for those inaccuracies.

It's more important to find the points of agreement that support mutual understanding than to over-focus on imprecise small details. Certainly take the time to get a better explanation if your partner's words can be taken different ways, just don't punish them for not speaking exactly the way you want them to.

◆　◆　◆

A common mistake is that we don't *ask* for what we want during our arguments. We just remain upset that we're not getting it. We're looking to be validated but our partner's caught up in explaining himself. He's operating with good intentions because he's trying to help us understand where he's coming from, but it's not what is needed most in that moment. Rather than staying frustrated, we need to *guide* our partner in the right direction. ("Is there anything about what I'm saying that you can validate for me?")

And even then, sometimes, we need to guide them *specifically* to how we want them to validate. (Listening: "I just need you to hear me out." Acknowledgement: "Do you understand why that was so upsetting to me?" Apology: "I need a sincere apology from you." Ownership: "Is there anything in what I'm saying that you can own?")

Some people will be hesitant with guiding because they want their partners' response to be authentic rather than something that came from them, but often partners are already trying to validate or resolve, they're just not doing it the way the other is looking for. Rather than to just let the partner flounder, becoming frustrated and angry with his own failed attempts to satisfy his partner, it's kinder to show him the way. It would be a better judge of his lack of sincerity if you led him to what you needed but he refused to provide it.

Remember, you're trying to function as a team, not play mind games with each other. No matter how long you've been together, you will still need to educate each other at times as to what validation path is most desired for that particular conversation. Because you are complex you don't always seek the same kind of validation, so you need to be realistic that your partner isn't a mind reader - help narrow the options for him.

◆　◆　◆

Stereotypically, men immediately try to problem solve when someone brings them an issue, skipping validation. However, many times, for women, *validation is the resolution that they are seeking.* Men will attempt to simplify the process by trying to jump to Step 4, but end up over-complicating things because all they really needed to do was to go to Step 2.

## Step 3. Explain the Issue

I say provide an explanation "if necessary" because sometimes an explanation really doesn't need to occur. If you know you were wrong you don't need to waste time explaining yourself - validating by taking ownership should be enough (and possibly resolving if an actual strategy is required).

For couples that get lost in marathon arguments, *circular explanations* are usually the cause. Circular explanations occur in three different forms, but they keep the argument going round and round, never really getting anywhere because the path to actual resolution keeps getting stalemated.

The first form of circular arguments sometimes occurs because there's an underlying assumption, by whoever the issue is directed at, that there must be a misunderstanding at the root of the issue. The natural thinking is that if our reasoning is understood, the misunderstanding pointed out, our partner will back down and the issue will resolve itself. Sometimes that is the way it works, but other times it doesn't because we're making it about our partner hearing us, when, for him in that moment, it's about us first hearing him.

The experience goes like this:

She identifies her issue by saying, "I'm upset with you because...(she presents her evidence)"

To which he responds (explaining), "You *shouldn't* be upset, because... (he presents his evidence)"

They each go back and forth adding more evidence to make their case, neither side feeling heard.

If she feels that she has a right to be upset, his telling her that she shouldn't isn't going to help move things forward. He just invalidated her. He may actually have a valid case, but it's not going to be heard until he validates her first. Remember, validation does *not* mean agreement.

◆　◆　◆

Second, for couples who play "the blame game", the circular argument is where each keeps pointing the finger back at the other.

For a couple that's been together for any significant period of time, each has a good deal of examples of where each has fallen short in the past. The blame game can be an attempt to balance our partner's perception by pointing out that he does the very thing he's accusing us of – that there's a double standard. But this natural tendency to counter our partner comes across as a deflection, which it may very well be.

An out-of-control blame game, where we keep piling on each other's faults to prove who is worse, ends up over-whelming the situation with issues that may not even be issues. And we have no idea how to start sorting it all out. And all either side feels is rejected.

You can't fairly address two issues at the same time. Whether or not your partner does what he's accusing you of, doesn't change the fact that, if he raised this issue, it's his issue with you, so he needs to have it addressed and resolved. Then it can be your turn, making the resolution that you agreed to with him into a rule for both.

◆　◆　◆

Third, for the bigger issues, couples go back and forth because the issue requires a solution for *both* partners. The struggle is over whose side of the issue gets validated and resolved first.

By raising the issue, she's making the issue about what she needs from him, which leads him to automatically think about what his need is of her with the same issue. And the reality is that the solution is going to have to address *both* needs, so it's going to have to have two parts.

She starts with, "I need you to be more caring."

To which he responds with, "Well, I would be more caring if you were more sensitive."

To which she counters, "Well, I would be more sensitive, if you were more caring."

To step out of the stalemate, *each* person's part of the issue needs to be addressed and explored, but *it starts with whoever brought it up to begin with*. She initially has the stage and her side needs to be validated, processed, and at least partially resolved, before it switches over to the partner. At which point, the partner's side of the issue takes center stage and now he gets his validation and resolution. One side at a time or it turns into a competition.

If they don't take turns this way, her experience of their conversation will be, "It's my issue but you keep making it about you."

## Step 4. Resolve the Issue

Does there always have to be a solution? No, not really. As I said in Step 2, sometimes validation is a resolution in itself. But, if the situation is a recurring one that requires change, more than just validation, specific problem-solving needs to take place if the cycle is to stop.

Just remember that you don't have to have all of the answers up front. It is more important to stay open to finding solutions together, and asking each other for help when the right words can't be found.

The biggest part of resolving the issue is focusing on *two-part solutions* – what she needs from him and what he needs from her.

In a relationship, there is no such thing as an individual issue, because his or her issues become *our* issues. Even if I'm the one with the anger problem, there are still things that my partner can do to help or hinder my issue. By trying to identify things that *both* of us can do to help whatever issues arise, we are staying with a team approach, avoiding the blame game.

By accepting joint ownership for the issues that arise, we are communicating the message, "I am not your enemy. I am your partner. We'll work this out together. We *each* play a part in the solution."

◆　◆　◆

Many people avoid conflict because they hate the discomfort of dealing with their partner's pain, or their own. But what they need to realize with avoiding going deeper with their conversations is that they're also losing emotional intimacy. As I pointed out earlier, you can't feel secure in a relationship if you know your partner can't handle your pain - the relationship develops a superficial feel to it. By avoiding validation and explanation, we lose a very important opportunity to better understand our partner's perspective. It's also an opportunity to show *them* that we understand it, respect it, and can still support them even when we don't completely agree with it.

Emotional intimacy may have been created initially by sharing the good times, but the foundation of a relationship is significantly strengthened by the intimacy gained when we're able to go through the difficult times and still remain respectful and considerate of each other.

## DVDs and Blu-rays

I will often suggest to couples to think of approaching the 4-step process with a DVD remote in your hand (or, for the tech-savvy, a blu-ray player). Unless it's a minor issue you don't want to hit the fast-forward button, but you do want to feel free to hit the rewind button as much as is needed. I don't say this in order to suggest that you keep re-hashing an issue, I mean rewinding back to the point in the conversation where things went wrong and attempting a do-over.

If the delivery was bad, you hit the rewind back to that point. He says, "Can you put your issue out there again but this time try to do it a little more gently, because it's hard not to take it as anything other than an attack." If she's so out-of-control that she can't do so, maybe now is not a good time to have a conversation - unless you're willing to give her the room to vent and the two of you can come back later to process it.

If validation is absent, it's hitting the rewind button again. She says, "I don't need you to solve this for me, I just need you to take the time to hear me out."

We're leading each other to the things that need a chance to be re-stated rather than just expecting them to get everything right the first time through.

Sometimes it's hitting the rewind button for ourselves. "Okay, let me start over. That was a crappy way to start the conversation, I admit it."

## The Best Relationship Question Ever

One of the most effective questions that is both validating and resolving is, "What do you feel that you need from me right now?"

You want to be careful that you don't use it too early in the conversation, however, because you don't want to convey that you're doing "the guy thing" and just trying to skip past the validation and processing piece of the conversation to solve things.

And you need to ask it with the right tone and sincerity, not with impatience and frustration.

"What do you *need* from me?" addresses the likelihood that if this issue is that upsetting, it is likely impacting a need, and you're willing to tend to that need.

"What do you need from me *right now*?" addresses those issues that have a history. Many times the current infraction is being connected to past events or old patterns of similar infractions. We are sometimes being loaded down with not only what just happened, but with things that happened weeks, months, or years ago that we can do nothing about in the moment.

She reacts with, "What I needed from you was not to have said that to my family *three years ago!*"

He reacts with, "What I needed from you was to not have embarrassed me at that party *6 months back!*"

To which we respond, "Yes, I understand that. But since I can't change history, what do you need from me *right now,* so that we can start moving forward again?"

By doing this, we stay focused on the present moment, the only thing that is actually in our control to do something about. For couples that get lost in over-exploring issues, or are stuck in circular explanations, it's a nice re-focusing tool that can get couples back on a positive track with where the conversation needs to go. Solution-focused versus problem-obsessed.

# Replays

I said at the beginning of this chapter, "the ideal progression for conflict resolution, *when it involves a deeper issue,* looks like this", because sometimes it *doesn't* involve a deeper issue and to get into a major discussion ends up making something small overly complicated, and mistakenly bigger than it is.

Part of knowing when to go deeper and when to stay on the surface comes back to attaching a value to the issue.

Let me use an example. Sometimes someone will be walking out the door of a relationship, fed up, and the partner is looking on in total surprise having no idea that things were that bad. It wasn't that the person walking out had never said anything, it was that she had never really attached a value to her issue. She had complained, yes, but it kind of sounded like all of her other complaints. So it got filed away in "the complaint drawer". It left it up to her partner to attach his own value to her issue. In his mind, "She's just complaining. She'll get over it."

I'll often ask couples to start attaching a value to their issues using a 1-10 scale. One being minimal and 10 being a deal-breaker. If either says an issue is a 5 or greater, then it's likely going to require a deeper discussion. If it's below a 5, then they can probably just do a *replay.*

Replays are solution-focused. It's not going to be a deeper discussion, it's simply going to be, "If we had to do it over again, what would you have needed differently from me?" And then, "This is what I needed different from you." Alternatives are identified, different approaches agreed on, and back to living life. For the smaller stuff, it doesn't have to get any more complicated.

## The Reactive Couple

There are two extremes when it comes to mental illness: taking on too much emotional pain (depression, neuroses) or avoiding it altogether (character disorders, psychoses). The reactive couple is doing a little bit of both - taking on too much pain by actively looking for offense with each other's behavior, and yet not taking responsibility for their own behavior, considering their own fault.

For the reactive couple (the couple that reacts to each other's reactions), there's a special dynamic that develops over time. Normally when a couple is having their first few arguments there is a gradual escalation to the negative emotion. It starts at neutral but then changes to frustrated. Frustrated raises to agitated. Agitated turns into angry. Angry moves to raging (if it ever gets that far). Usually when this negative pattern is starting it takes many encounters before it ever gets to the "raging" level.

But because the reactive couple is now quite practiced in moving through this negative emotional ladder, the over-familiarity with the pattern leads them to begin skipping steps. The normal course of escalation is now greatly accelerated because they go straight from neutral to angry. Because of how quickly it becomes intensely emotional, it leaves little opportunity for an actual intelligent conversation.

The reactive couple no longer takes turns with the tennis back-and-forth interaction, and so things quickly become chaotic and competitive. Prior to this you usually see some attempts to balance conversations - he's upset so she soothes, or vice versa. But when things have become reactive there is no longer any balance, *both* are going with instinct and fall into attack or angry withdrawal mode.

When the relationship has deteriorated to this point, the couple has to intentionally start *slowing the conversation down* again in order to have more opportunities to think about what the partner is saying, and what they're about to say - to take back control. So long as it remains the fast paced no-holds-barred approach, there's no time for anything to be constructively edited or thought through.

One tool for restoring a sequence to the conversations (taking turns) is to use an identified object, such as a pillow. Whoever is the holder of the pillow "has the floor". When he's done with what he has to say, it gets passed on. If the holder of the pillow is being a Child, he may refuse to give it up. Or, if he's being the Parent, he may try to turn the pillow privilege into a lecture, or a monologue. But you're trying to work at being Adults, so be nice with the pillow and share.

Reactive couples need to have conversations in terms of approach-retreat, taking time before they jump into an issue to think things through, focusing on staying with the issue and managing their own reactions (not the partner's), and taking a healthy exit if things start to get too intense. Then they try again. The initial goals are simply to keep it slow, regain some control of the reactions, and know when to step away. Baby steps.

## The Avoidant Couple

The opposite of the reactive couple is the couple that constantly *avoids* conflict – those who withdraw or seek flight. It goes counter to many people's sensibilities that in order to find happiness in your relationship you need to be *willing* to experience pain. The avoidant couple avoids the pain of perceived conflict, yet also takes on too much imagined pain for how their partners might react.

Perhaps they never saw their own parents argue. Or perhaps that is all they saw and so their way of dealing with the pain they were exposed to as a child was to retreat altogether. But *the ways we coped with life as a child will not usually work as an adult. Adult life works by different rules.*

The avoidant couple often avoids conflict because they see "raising an issue" as being synonymous with "starting an argument". For them, approaching conflict is being intentionally hurtful, and they don't want to be mean. So while their actions frequently come from good intentions in the moment, the "kindness" of their withholding, in the long run, actually ends up hurting the relationship, just not as openly.

They typically recognize only two ways of relating - the extremes of *passive* (I lose but you win) or *aggressive* (I win but at the cost of you losing). To be aggressive is seen as selfish – one putting his own needs first. But they fail to recognize that there is an ideal middle ground called *assertive* where we can respectfully address our issues, and *both* sides win. Even if they do recognize that assertive exists, the projected discomfort of walking that verbal tightrope is enough to keep avoidant couples from trying.

On the surface, the couple that actively seeks flight can look very healthy. The *absence* of conflict is automatically assumed by many to indicate things are going well for them. For the couple themselves, this *illusion* of health can be enough to maintain the relationship for quite a while, because of their own need to see everything as okay.

It makes sense that this kind of couple usually takes longer to reach a crisis point, and longer to get to the point where change is seen to be necessary, simply because the relationship is about maintaining peace at all costs. The reactive couple is much more likely to bring things to a head in a much shorter time. Their constant conflict, if not resolved or given space, naturally leads to a crisis. The avoidant couple, however, is working actively to prevent this from happening. Any crisis is soothed by the act of silence, minimizing or denial. It's unusual since sometimes it is not just *one* person withdrawing and the other resenting him for it; *both* sides can often be in a sort of collusion to maintain the peace.

I'm not referring to those couples that have learned to accept each other's petty differences (which is a healthy thing), but rather those couples whose needs aren't being met who just pretend they're okay when they're not.

Seeking counseling for such a couple is often unlikely since the idea of talking about private things openly, things that could possibly be painful, is actively stepping out against the tradition of the relationship. This is why at least one person in the relationship has to have the insight to recognize that avoidance is not working, and that they very much want the relationship to work – enough that they are willing to risk the pain of honesty and vulnerability.

One of the underlying dilemmas with the avoidant couple is that, because they *don't* share uncomfortable information, they are still making assumptions of each other but never attempting to find out if those assumptions are accurate. As a result, their understanding of each other can become quite distorted. Their positive behavior creates a sense of closeness, but because the verbal intimacy that does occur is only a partial truth, they can still be growing apart without even realizing it.

If they can come to understand that conflict doesn't have to be a negative, that there is such a thing as *constructive criticism*, they're more likely to start venturing into that fearful but necessary territory. The approach-retreat ritual that the reactive couple takes becomes the same path for the avoidant couple. They practice sharing necessary information in a respectful way, seeing that they can do it safely without the imagined harm, and learn to find their own voice in the relationship.

------

There's a lot of information in these first two chapters and I understand that it can be overwhelming the first time through. If I had to summarize it, it would come down to these five key tools of conflict resolution:

1.  Remembering to give the benefit of the doubt, rather than to assume or feed a conspiracy theory
2.  Staying with sincere questions ("How did you interpret what I said?", "Why was that so upsetting for you?", "What do you need from me right now?")
3.  Taking the time to validate (listen, acknowledge, apologize, own)
4.  Working towards 2-part solutions
5.  Knowing when to take healthy exits

For the majority of couples who do not reach workable solutions, it is usually due to at least one of these five points being ignored or forgotten. Try to view them as tools to bring into play when you're trying to work through things with your partner. If you're getting lost in an argument, stop for a moment and ask yourself which of these tools would be the most helpful. Even if you don't know which one might be the best in that moment, at least you've got options you can try.

◆　◆　◆

The next four chapters are going to go into more detail on the four stages of moving through an issue (Identify, Validate, Process and Resolve). Each has particular strategies that overlap to a degree with the other stages. What I would suggest is taking a look at the "ABC's for a Fair Fight" in the Appendices at the end of this book. This is a summary of the 26 points that will be covered in those four chapters. What some couples will do is identify for themselves which of the 26 points are their own trouble areas, and then focus on the corresponding sections as they go back to the reading.

## Summary Points:

1.  Keep in mind the four stages of resolution: 1) *identifying* the issue, 2) *validating* each other, 3) *explaining* any misunderstandings or exploring the issue with additional relevant information, and 4) moving on to a solution (*resolving*).

2.  With identifying, try not to get in the habit of waiting to raise issues at the point that you're really upset. Your delivery sets the stage for whether or not the conversation has a chance of going well.

3.  Validation is the step most likely to be skipped in a conflict, keeping the couple from reaching a resolution. It consists of active listening, acknowledging, apologizing and taking ownership.

4.  Try to stay focused on *two-part solutions* for the bigger issues, since both of you play a part, even when it's an individual issue.

5.  If it's your issue, remember to guide your partner to what you need, not expect them to just know it.

6.  You gain emotional intimacy by being able to go deeper with your issues. The key is to keep it respectful and considerate.

7. Not all issues require all 4 steps. For smaller issues, doing a replay focusing just on a better solution for each would be sufficient.

8. "What do you need from me right now?" is one of the best questions for both validation and resolution if the conversation starts to become circular or not going anywhere.

9. A reactive couple reacts to each other's reactions – each giving up his control, waiting on the other to do the right thing first. Don't wait for your partner to be the first to "do the right thing", model what you want.

10. The avoidant couple actively avoids issues but is actually neglecting the health of the relationship, often due to good intentions.

## Discussion Questions:

1. **Where does your relationship get stuck? Identifying, validating, explaining or resolving?** How do you plan on improving those blind spots?

2. **Why is validating so difficult to do, and so easy to forget?** How are you going to do a better job of remembering it?

3. **How actively do you work towards two-part solutions, where each person accepts a part in the solution?**

4. **Why is it important to attach a value to your issues?**

5. **How is emotional intimacy gained by taking the time to validate and process?**

6. **What is the difference between a replay and the 4 steps?**

# Chapter 3
# Identifying the Issue

The tools for conflict resolution are deceptively simple and it is perhaps because of this simplicity that they are often overlooked. Just because many of them are basic does not make them easily remembered, or easy to use in the heat of the moment. You can say, "Well, of course, I know that listening is important", and you may feel that you do it all of the time, but do you do it in a way that helps your partner feel that he's really been heard? After all, when you're in an emotional struggle with someone you care a great deal about, it is very hard to stay rooted in common sense.

Identifying an issue is that delicate territory where we have to decide how we're going to bring up an issue to our partner – not just letting him know we're upset, but *why* we're upset. Of course, many of us don't give it too much consideration – something upsets us and we launch right into expressing our emotions, never stopping to think about what we're going to say or how we're going to say it – like putting a car into "drive" before we've even given ourselves a chance to get behind the wheel.

So let me make a few suggestions for where to head when you first *do* take the wheel.

**Betty walks into the room upset. Bob's sitting on the couch reading the newspaper. Betty says, "Bob, this is really bothering me. Whenever I try to talk to you, you don't listen. I'm trying to communicate with**

you and you're off in your own world, acting like you're listening when you're not."

Bob, looking up from the newspaper, responds, "Honey, you're always wanting to talk! There's no way I can possibly listen to all of it. Even when I do listen, it never seems to be enough. I don't know what you want from me!"

Betty says, "Well, I want to feel like you care enough about me to listen!"

---

## Rule #1. Choose your battles, and battlefield, wisely.

---

I know that using the word "battle" sounds overly dramatic and casts resolution in a negative light, but give me some room to explain. You've probably heard variations of the phrase, "What good is winning a battle, if you lose the war." For relationships, it makes the point that sometimes we get so caught up in winning the battle, the fight at hand, that we fail to see the long-term impact that these battles are having.

Ideally, the goal of winning a war in the real world is to restore peace. For a couple, the goal of the "war" is the survival of the relationship – to win your freedom from unhealthy past alliances (emotional baggage), to quell whatever rebellions start within the ranks (the struggles over self), and to unite your forces for a common good (working as a team to deal with life's stresses). To "lose the war" is to destroy what keeps the couple connected – by letting history get in the way of the present, self come before "us", and circumstances to distract and divide.

The war is *not* against your partner; it's against everything that threatens or can harm the relationship. Because sometimes it *is* your partner, or you, that is endangering the relationship, some of the battles will be between you and him, but the war itself starts out with the two of you on the same side. Thinking in these terms, it's important that when we approach these "battles", the focus is on restoring the healthy alliance, not pushing our partner further into the role of enemy.

We need to take the time to consider the weight of our issues before we just let off a cannonball volley at our partner. Is this something really worth getting into, or are there better things for us to be focusing on?

Often, in the moment, what seems like an issue isn't that big a deal a day later. In the scheme of things, it would have been better to let it pass by as the temporary annoyance that it was - or maybe to mildly educate your partner, rather than to initiate an attack.

By saying this, I'm not promoting neglect. I'm not saying ignore voicing your needs. But I do want to caution you not to make every little thing into a big thing.

Some people are critical by nature, and part of their everyday conversation is to judge and critique. To them, doing so may be considered nothing – just passing observations of the things that annoy them. Or it may just be that they're very into improving the relationship and they see another area for potential growth. But to their partners, this chronic "complaining" can have a very negative impact, wearing away at their peace and creating resentment. To them, the critic is constantly seeking battles – never satisfied, never content.

We need to be *thinking* consciously of the big picture rather than becoming lost in the *feeling* of the moment. And if we're so close to it that we can't see the big picture, usually it means that we need to take some time to step back from it so that we can.

For Betty, she'd had a lot of time to think about things. There was a recurring pattern going on with Bob that needed to be addressed. The issue was relevant in terms of the quality of their relationship, both now and for the future. The "battle" was a necessary one.

◆　◆　◆

In terms of battle*fields*, before we start discussing an issue, we need to take a moment to consider the setting - the "where" and the "when" the conversation is to take place.

Bob and Betty's setting is in their home, in the living room - a natural place for a discussion to occur. The "where" is okay, or is it? The TV may be on, or the radio, kids may be running through the house.

Sometimes people have a tendency to bring up serious issues in the wrong places – where there are distractions, kids who don't need to be exposed to the intimate details of the relationship, friends or family embarrassed. We don't need to interrupt a positive activity and ruin it by raising an issue. Some people want to deal with issues as they occur to them, regardless of the setting, and they need to rethink this habit if they want to get positive results. *If you want focused attention, choose a place where you're most likely to get it.*

What about the "when"? If you asked Bob, in the middle of reading his newspaper, it probably wasn't a good time. (Of course, Betty might respond "Well, there's *never* a good time for Bob.") I didn't say whether it was on the weekend or during the workweek. If Bob was just relaxing, unwinding after a day at the office, it probably would have been better for Betty to wait until later in the evening. The reason for this may not be so obvious. *If Bob's repeated experience of coming home is that he gets hit with problems soon after he gets through the door, Betty's shaping Bob to dread coming home.*

While Betty's needs *are* important, it's just as important to pick a time when those needs are more likely to be heard. Bob's still mentally dumping the problems from work and trying to get some space from his day. Bob's trying to de-stress and Betty's putting more on him. Now, I'm not trying to make Betty the bad guy. She may have had a hard day too. But rather than finding out first if now is a good time to talk, she jumps right in. If she wants to be heard, she needs to find out first if now is a good time for Bob to listen.

If Bob has a tendency to say "not now" but "later" never happens, then he's asking for Betty to force things. Otherwise, asking is a simple sign of respect. And the person asking needs to be shown respect in return. If "now" is truly not a good time for Bob, then he needs to commit to a time that *would* work, rather than just leave the issue hanging.

Another time people often pick to discuss issues is just before bedtime. While some people just *have* to talk about an issue, because if they don't they won't be able to sleep, they need to choose a time where there's less need to rush through the conversation. Besides, usually if you're ready to sleep, your mind is not at its sharpest.

Of course, there are times when it's just not convenient but things still need to be said. You may have to settle for not getting the full attention of your partner. Or he may have to drop what he's doing out of respect for your need. The point that I'm trying to get across, however, is that if you have the luxury of being able to think ahead, choose the time and the place carefully if you want an optimal solution and optimal responsiveness. If the issue is an important one to you, you want to approach it with the greatest chances for success.

When we get to Chapter 9 on healthy routines, having an accountability routine where the couple regularly sits down and discusses both the positive and the not-so-positive becomes a platform to regularly voice concerns. Having such a routine provides a place for the couple to discuss their issues so now issues don't have to creep into all of the other conversations. There's a time and a place reserved.

---

## Rule #2. Identify the purpose of approaching a conversation to your partner. Don't assume that he knows it.

---

Rule #2 addresses the "why" we're starting an issue. Looking at Betty and Bob's conversation, note that nobody's actually being hostile. Nobody's trying to hurt the other. Betty's sharing a concern and Bob's responding. Nobody's abusing anybody. It's a relatively harmless interaction with no grievous errors. But let me make a few comments about this conversation. Betty *does* want more than just a listening ear. Betty probably wants different things at different times. While some times it is probably just about being heard, other times she probably wants assurance. Sometimes she may want resolution. In this instance, she probably wants a variety of things but, mainly, she is seeking a resolution to a recurring problem.

The greater error with just jumping into an issue without knowing what we want is expecting our partner to know what we want when we don't know it ourselves.

More often, we have an *intent* but we don't flag it for our partner; we just expect them to know what it is we're looking for. One word for this is *egocentric* – when we assume that others are automatically aware of what we mean because *we* know what we mean. If we're able to let our partner know what we need from him up front, he won't have to be put in the position of being a mind-reader.

*It's more important that the initiator express what he needs from the conversation rather than complaining about what he doesn't.*

She says, "Don't solve this for me."

He responds with, "Okay, you *don't* want a solution but what *do* you want?"

Betty needs to identify for Bob what she is looking for from him with this particular conversation: a listening ear, help with a problem, support, ownership, whatever. Let's say she does it "by the book". This time she starts with "Bob, I've got a concern that's been bothering me and I need your help in resolving it."

She's letting him know she needs more than eye contact and a nod. She isn't starting off with an attack. She is inviting his input and needs a resolution to the issue.

If Bob's doing his part in this, he now has some sense of direction. He can reach for those problem-solving skills guys like to wield so often. If Bob only apologizes but a plan is being sought, then Betty needs to let him know she needs more than just an apology. If Bob complies but only offers a plan that says what Betty can do different, then she's going to need to let him know that she needs something different from him as well.

When couples are in sync, you don't have to point out what you need every time. However, if you notice you're either not being heard correctly or your partner is trying to help but missing the point, take the time to stop and explain what you want rather than walking away frustrated.

---

**Rule #3. Confrontation is based on facts. Don't confront based on fears and doubts.**

---

With inappropriate confrontation, we are telling our partner what they have done, *without* the facts to support it. We are going on a hunch, a fear, a guess, a possible pattern of behavior, or a leap of logic. But if we are tempted to confront based on our fears and doubts, then *what we need to do first is seek information in order to get our facts straight.*

What we often really need is *assurance* – about love, trust, fidelity, etc. However, because this is seen as a position of "neediness", or weakness, it is often avoided.

One of the basic principles for dealing with any situations where our concerns are based on fears and doubts, not facts, is to identify them for what they are. We don't need to keep them to ourselves, but we also don't need to approach our partner as if our fears are realities.

If we accuse him of something he didn't do, but we're *afraid* that he might have, then we are essentially calling him a liar and directly attacking the trust of the relationship.

If we express it as a fear, "Honey, I don't know if this is just me or what, but I'm feeling like you're drifting, that you're losing interest in us", then we are identifying it as a feeling, not saying it's a fact, giving them the *benefit of the doubt* and inviting assurance if it's not true.

If we find that we continue to need frequent assurance *despite* no further evidence for our fear then, hopefully, we will start to see that our own insecurity is the problem.

Now some people would say that this is being naïve and leaving the other person to take advantage simply by saying "Oh, no, honey, everything's fine" when it may not be. While it's true it does leave us open to be taken advantage of, this is our partner we're talking about. Part of the definition of any significant personal relationship is the willingness to be vulnerable – the willingness to risk out of trust. It's choosing to take the moral high road. Better to trust and be wrong than to not trust and, as a result, never have a relationship where you can be truly close because you are unable to risk being hurt.[4]

◆   ◆   ◆

Confrontation, when it does take place, works best if it is done in a loving manner, not a judgmental one. It is not done to hurt or to punish; *it is done to hold your partner accountable to his commitment towards the relationship.* Part of the process may involve sharing your pain over the wrong done, but its' intent is not to commit an additional wrong by attacking.

A lot of the early models for counseling substance abuse clients were around constant confrontation since much of the initial problem with treating the disease is the continuing denial that exists both at the start and throughout treatment. Confrontation, however, works best when you've already established a relationship with the client and there's some level of trust that's been earned. In other words, if I've accepted that the confrontation is occurring because this other person cares about me and

---

[4]   There *are* people who continually choose bad relationships and trust all the wrong people. For those folks, discretion and evidence should play a more central role in their relationships than the norm.

he's trying to help, I'm going to be much more open to hearing it rather than reacting to it. To step in and tell someone that he's lying when you really haven't earned the "right" to do so, even *with* the facts to back it up, often just pushes the accused to shut down.

The approach I like the best is the "Columbo" model, taking the Peter Faulk role of confused detective. You take what your partner's saying and you share your confusion over the difference between two contradictory statements or the discrepancy between something he's done versus what he's said. It's usually phrased like "I'm not sure I'm hearing you right (scratching head). Are you saying that…?" You're not making any accusations but you're letting him see you're noticing the discrepancy. It's then up to him to own up to things or provide an explanation, but it's done in a way where you've pretty much led him to the water and it's now up to him to assume responsibility for taking the drink.

What Betty did with Bob was a mild confrontation. She called him on the times that had occurred when he had failed to attend to her. This was based on actual past occurrences, not her fears that at some point he may not listen. She did start to make some inferences from this about his not caring which started to miss the mark, but the initial confrontation was over factual events.

◆   ◆   ◆

We have to be careful about generalizing a *pattern* of problems too broadly when we are pointing out a problematic "theme" to our partner. While we may not share the same specific problems that our partner has, *when we start to broaden the scope of the problem that we're addressing, often it will start to encompass areas that we ourselves have difficulties in.*

For example, let's say we are approaching our partner about not being disciplined enough in managing the finances, essentially creating a threat to our financial security. It would be a mistake to address it as a lack of discipline, rather than a *specific* problem with managing the finances, since we *all* have areas where we're not disciplined.

◆   ◆   ◆

There is a particular phenomenon that occurs sometimes when we question our partners. The more we question them, the deeper we go with an issue, we may start to get different answers of explanation. Sometimes this is because we've exposed a lie, but sometimes this is because we're starting to discover the complexity of the issue.

If we start with just a surface conversation, we get a simplified explanation.

He says, "You didn't get home when you said would last night."

She responds with, "I lost track of time. Sorry about that."

So her simplest explanation is that she was late due to being distracted.

He presses, "So what was going on?"

"When I was out shopping, I added some things to my list that I hadn't initially thought of."

So now the explanation is both distracted and a longer shopping list than expected.

"You didn't tell me you were going to go shopping," he replies, a little upset. "You said you were running late with work."

"I was," she defends. "And on my way home, I thought of some things we needed."

So now it's distracted, longer shopping list than expected, running late from work.

"So you lied to me," he insists. "You never told me about the shopping until now."

"You didn't ask for details until now," she says, getting upset herself. "Why should I have to tell you every little thing I do? We're adults! Are you saying you don't trust me that I was actually shopping?"

Obviously he has his own conspiracy theory about the real issue, and maybe there's a history of her withholding information. But without such a history, this is simply a matter of finally having a more detailed conversation about what happened last night. The more in-depth the conversation gets, the more details will come out. No one detail has to be the whole truth, each detail can actually be part of what makes up the whole.

Remembering that each of us, and our situations, can be more complicated at times than we get credit for, if we can hang on to the benefit of the doubt, we can handle the likelihood that the deeper we go with an issue, the more factors we're going to uncover that contributed to the issue. Rarely do we do any one thing for just one reason.

When it comes to lies, the things we're concerned with is when there's contradictions when more details are added.

"Wait a minute, you said you were at Susan's last night. Now you're saying you were at Sarah's. Which is it?"

◆　◆　◆

Part of learning each other's personalities and "language" is learning how to confront so that the other can receive it. And what that looks like from couple to couple will differ. How we discover the styles that work is through trial and error and through asking our partner for his help with the ongoing education. The error is in the extremes - when confrontation is avoided at all costs, or when it occurs so frequently that it loses all meaning or becomes constant rejection.

## Rule #4. Attach a priority to issues, so there is some sense of how important or unimportant an issue is.

As I mentioned in Chapter 2, when it's at the point that one partner is walking out the door of the relationship that the other suddenly starts to pay attention, the problem can sometimes not be an insensitive partner, but the *overly familiar pattern of confrontation.*

If your partner becomes used to you regularly complaining, after a while, the issues tend to take on a similar drone to him. If you complain about everything to the same degree, not identifying for your partner which issues are big and which ones are small, it leaves it up to him to assign his own priority to them. They all go into the same "complaint drawer".

When the partner was finally walking out the door, the one being left suddenly became attentive because it wasn't until then that it was made clear to him just how important her issues were for her. Prior to that, while he probably did notice when she was venting, he still thought that the relationship itself was secure.

In the same way that as parents we need to teach our children what wrongs and rights are more important than others, we also need to accurately communicate what issues are priorities for us in our relationships. ("On a scale of 1 to 10, this is an 8 for me.")

Betty attempted to let Bob know that her issue was an important one to her. ("Bob, this is really bothering me.") Bob, by explaining himself, was attempting to dismiss her issue, or get her to understand his side of the problem, but he was failing to validate things for Betty. She would have to go on to let him know that her issue required a solution more than a defense. (She might say, "I understand there're complications to this, but this isn't something I can just accept as not going to change. We need to talk this through to what we can do differently. It's that important to me.")

If our partner feels that our issue is over "nothing", then we need to be able to identify that it may be "nothing" for him, but definitely "something" for us.

We need to recognize that "all issues aren't created equal". Some issues are minor, and others are big. We don't want our partner thinking that all our issues are big ones or we become deserving of the label "high maintenance". If just about everything *is* "something" for us, then we might need to learn to get a better perspective on what is worth getting that upset about.

Some will hesitate to label minor issues "minor", thinking that if they do it will continue to be ignored. But, as with needs, the couple should have a clear sense of what issues are more important for each person.

---

**Rule #5. Bringing up the negative past during an argument should be done only if the problem is continuing to occur.**

---

There is no Relationship 101 that we are required to take while growing up. Yet when we enter into a relationship or a marriage, we seem to expect that each of us should automatically know what to do. And we make judgments about each other when we don't. If we viewed relationships as learning experiences, and the start of each as time to educate each other rather than assuming we were already supposed to know all of that, expectations would probably be a lot more realistic. Solid relationships are created over time; they don't just fall into our laps.

One of the biggest "beginner" mistakes in communication has to do with how couples handle bringing up the past. There are exceptions to this rule, but let's talk about why the rule exists first before we look at when it shouldn't. Typically, the past is used as a tool to punish rather than a tool to gain understanding. How can we keep a positive environment in our relationship if we are using attack strategies? And how can we develop a mature relationship if we are engaging in childish mud-slinging?

Let's say something has happened in the past, maybe several years ago, that has been traumatic to the degree that it has wounded the relationship. One partner seriously wronged the other. Let's also assume that the same situation has not occurred since, but trust issues continue to be a significant part of the relationship. Maybe the trust issues now are around finances, or taking each other at his word. It would be predictable, but unwise, that when issues become heated that that past traumatic event will ultimately be brought up as "the big gun", since it is connected to the damaged trust. In this situation, *the traumatic event becomes a way for the injured partner to always be in a superior position* – there is nothing that the other can do to erase the past and so he is always helpless to defend himself. But to continue to use this as leverage in arguments undermines any act of forgiveness that hopefully occurred concerning the past wrong.

Now we may say that the past event *was* connected to the other issues because it is all trust-related, so why not bring it up again? But even if that is where the trust issues originated, usually both sides are so aware of its having happened and the pain it involved that *there is no need* to bring it up again – everyone knows where it started. Continuing to bring it up only turns the focus of attention off the current issues and onto you for being "harassing" or "unforgiving".

Continuing to resurrect old issues for ammunition in the present is working against the relationship moving forward by anchoring it to the past.

◆ ◆ ◆

Bringing up the past can often side-track the current issue. The conversation is going along well, both sides taking turns and hearing the other out, when suddenly somebody references something that happened just a month ago. It automatically shifts the attention away from talking about the present issue and leads the other to believe that this other event needs worked through as well – so now we're not just dealing with what happened today, but last month, too. We're starting to stack up issues or events. And the conversation starts to get overly complicated. It might be helpful to stop and say "Wait a minute. Is that something that still needs worked through too or are you just using it as an example?" in order to clarify what the other's wanting.

◆　◆　◆

Using the past frequently can give a negative sense of record-keeping to the relationship. Record-keeping gives the message that we are not being forgiven for our past mistakes. It makes us feel like we are living with a disapproving parent who is keeping lists on us. Now if we are acting like an irresponsible child in the relationship, expecting there to be no accountability, then maybe we *are* forcing our partner into this role.

Typically, lists go along with judgments. We use them as barrages to overwhelm our partner about what a horrible person he is. She calls him a "failure" or "lazy" (insert insult of choice) and then goes into her long list of past wrongs to substantiate just how much of one he is. As we'll discuss later concerning judgments, we are operating in delicate territory when we attack our partner's character as it leaves little room for a positive outcome and a continuing relationship. If we want to be effective in motivating change, we need to be more selective in how we use the past.

Betty identified to Bob that the problems had been recurring. However, she did not go into detail about when and where, *and there was no need to*, since Bob wasn't arguing the point. He did counter her issue with a rationale, but he didn't deny that her perception was accurate so there was no need to reach for more evidence. *Don't go for overkill to make a point if the point has already been acknowledged – focus on working out the resolution.*

◆　◆　◆

Let's define some of the specifics of "only if the problem is continuing to occur", or when bringing up the past is justified.

1. If the significance of a problem is being denied or dismissed, we can use past events to support the point we are trying to make, showing our

partner that it is not just a current, isolated event but something that has happened before. The intent is to create a basis for our argument. Note that much of our success in getting this across will have to do with our tone, our body language and our delivery.

2. Using the past is most helpful when our partner is requesting more information in order to better understand our issue or concern.

3. *Always* feel free to bring up the past in order to give recognition for things done well or things appreciated. It's much more beneficial to the relationship to be keeping a list of the successes rather than the failures.

---

Each "rule", used well, requires a good deal of restraint, humility, and emotional maturity. It's tough to swallow pride. It's difficult to think when we're upset. It's hard to refrain from verbally striking back when we've been hurt. It ain't easy!

Successful application of the rules requires practice, and they need fine-tuning to fit each relationship, but they get better results than if we ignore them and go with what comes naturally. Doing the work of using the "rules", choosing the more difficult but mature path, allows us to retain our integrity during times when integrity tends to be lacking.

## Summary Points:

1.  Choose your battles, and battlefield, wisely. Pay attention to the time and place you choose to discuss an issue. Be sure that the issue is important enough that it requires discussion.

2.  Identify the intent of approaching a conversation to your partner; don't assume that he knows it. Do you simply want a listening ear, to share your feelings, to get feedback, or are you wanting to resolve an issue? It helps to identify what you are looking for before you get into a conversation. That way you avoid guesswork on the other's part and you are more likely to get your need met.

3. Confrontation is based on facts. Don't confront based on fears and doubts. Fears and doubts are based on *possible* or *suspected* occurrences, not *known* occurrences. Confrontation only works if it is done in a loving manner, not a judgmental one. If you are tempted to confront based on your fears and doubts, then, what you probably need to do is seek information *first* in order to get your facts straight. What we often *truly* need is assurance – about love, trust, fidelity, etc.

4. If necessary, attach a priority to the issue, so there is some sense of how important or unimportant it is. When a lot of issues are being identified, it's important that there is some sense of scale to it all or the list will feel overwhelming. If needs are going to be met, each partner needs to have some sense of which issues require a focused priority.

5. Bring up the negative past during an argument only if the problem is continuing to occur. Occasionally, there will be a past issue that has gone unresolved and felt to be a major contributor to the present mood of the relationship whether or not that situation has re-occurred. In situations like that, a re-approach is justified. However, in general, it is unfair to bring up the distant past since it distracts the focus from current issues, and is often used as a way to punish the partner.

## Discussion Questions:

1. **Of these first 5 "rules", which ones do you have the most difficulty with?** Why?

2. **How are you going to put the rules that are most often ignored on such a conscious level that they are being applied when issues are being discussed?**

# Chapter 4
# Validating the Issue

Validation is the most frequently missed step in the resolution stages, and so couples go back and forth between re-stating the issue, and re-explaining their sides.

Reactive couples have this angry, verbal ping-pong match going on where the only thing they take turns with is finding new ways to be offended. Each person keeps making the issue all about them rather than taking the time to focus on one partner's issue at a time. Validation, a respect for perspective, is absent from the conversation.

Validation attempts to move us out of our reactive mind-set and think beyond our own internal perspective, restoring a balanced focus.

**Peter and Patty were in their mid-20's and had been dating for 8 months. Their concern was that there was a recurring theme of doing marathon discussions with the few problems the relationship had encountered. They were concerned that even though the problem count wasn't very high, they weren't able to resolve the few problems that there were.**

**"We just keep re-hashing the problem," said Peter. "It's not like we don't spend the time talking it out, it's just that we don't get anywhere."**

**"Peter doesn't hear me," said Patty. "I'll explain to him my concerns, but he thinks I should just get over it."**

"I don't expect you to just 'get over it', but I want you to accept what I say in return," responded Peter.

"For example?" I asked.

Peter looked to Patty.

"We were at a picnic last weekend," explained Patty. "And I was feeling like Peter was in a bad mood. He wasn't saying much and he didn't seem to be trying to spend much time with me. I thought he was angry at me, so I approached him about it, and he denied it. So I let it go, but he never came out of it. I approached him again later, and he denied it again, but I could tell he was upset with me for continuing to ask. So I let it go, but the rest of the day was ruined.

"I tried to talk about it again the next day, but Peter just acted like I was the problem and I should have just not said anything after the first time he said he was okay."

"I'd had a hard week at work and I wasn't really feeling sociable," said Peter. "I'd told her before that I didn't really feel up to going to the picnic. But I wasn't angry at Patty. She kept pushing me, insisting I must be angry with her, when I wasn't. Finally, I did become angry at her."

"I told you, you didn't have to go," inserted Patty.

"Yes, but I knew it would have disappointed you if I'd stayed at home," said Peter.

"It didn't make my day any better by you going and moping around," added Patty.

"And that's just it," replied Peter. "Part of my issue with her is that no matter what I do it doesn't seem like it's good enough."

## Rule #6. Balance the negative with the positive.

Think, for a moment, on how your parents motivated you as a child. Typically, it was based around consequences if resistance was encountered. If you did not do "such and such", something bad was going to happen – whether it was your father was going to be told, privileges were going to be removed, spankings would occur, disapproval and guilt were going to be handed out, lectures would occur, etc. Most children grow up learning that, to motivate another to do something, there need to be negative consequences attached. And so, as adults, we try to motivate each other by attaching punishments, lectures, and judgments in order to get compliance – in other words, we use parenting tactics.

We initially attract others through our unconditional regard and approval of who they are, only to later push them away through our rejection of the things we now voice our disapproval of. But *our primary focus needs to remain on reinforcing the positives, the small successes, as they occur.* If the relationship has deteriorated to a great degree, finding and reinforcing the positives can be difficult since we may first have to retrain ourselves to see where the positives still exist.

Since our initial response to criticism is usually to explain or defend ourselves, it's a positive strategy to enter into the conversation already providing for our partner's defense. When you approach him about an issue, try to think of a few positives to share first so he can see that you recognize there are good things happening too, and that you understand there are reasons for his behavior - though that doesn't necessarily excuse the behavior.

One form of this is trying to think about what some of your partner's reasons may be for his part of the problem - and validating them.

Patty, upon finding out that Peter had a hard work week, and really had made a personal sacrifice to come to the picnic, could have used that at some time during their discussion later. For example, "Peter, I do appreciate the fact that you were already stressed from work and still came to the picnic. I understand that you were doing that for me, and that means a lot. You're right, part of my concern was that you were angry with me, and it's good to know that that wasn't the case."

Since Peter's relating he doesn't feel appreciated for his sacrifices, Patty's validating that for him by recognizing his sacrifice as being important to her. She essentially just took part of his argument away from him, and, at the same time, did a half-decent job of not attacking.

She could have also reached for past successes. For example, "Peter, we've had many times together in the past, socially, where you were wonderful. Because this time was so out of character for you, it stood out to me and made me concerned."

Not only in this statement is she giving him credit for typically *not* being a social problem, she's also bringing her heart into it by expressing her reason for concern, rather than judging him for his behavior.

Patty can then move on to tell Peter what she's needing from him.

Unless Peter is paranoid and suspects a hidden agenda, he will probably respond positively to this approach. The difficulty, of course, is in being able to maintain this non-adversarial role throughout the rest of the resolution process.

◆　◆　◆

In couple's counseling, if someone is stuck in his own perception of an issue, counselors will sometimes have the couple switch roles and try to argue the point of view from the partner's perspective. While this can get twisted and used as an opportunity to bash the other, it can also be a very positive opportunity to think through what the logic and feelings of your partner might be. We are all too used to seeing things from *our* point of view - how interesting and, hopefully, educational to try to reason from someone else's.

◆　◆　◆

It's an interesting phenomenon that, in healthy relationships, we tend to automatically try to create balance in a relationship when it's being threatened. If you are pointing out the negative about something, the natural tendency for your partner is to try to balance it by recognizing the positives, and vice versa.

If you are really irritated with a family member, upset by something she said, and share that with your partner, it's natural for him to try to alleviate some of your irritation by presenting a less negative perspective ("She probably didn't mean that." "Maybe she was just having a bad day.") rather than to feed into it. But you have to be careful with this because, *in an effort to balance each other, you can often unintentionally be invalidating.* If your partner is wanting to vent about a family member and you try to rationalize the family member's point of view, the message you may be giving to your partner is that you're not supporting her. This goes back to Rule #2 to identify what you're looking for ("I don't need an alternative viewpoint right now, okay? I just need you to let me vent and be supportive.").

This natural tendency to balance works when you verbally recognize your partner's strengths – it frees him to examine his own weaknesses.

She says, "You really did a good job with putting me first last night. I appreciate that."

He responds with, "Thanks. I know I need to be more consistent with doing that."

By us defending or supporting our partners, they don't feel as much of a need to self-protect. Because they see that we're paying attention to their successes, they don't feel that they have to point them out. You are setting a positive pattern for the relationship – one of support, inspiration and growth that has a ripple effect into the other areas of the relationship.

*Couples who get caught up in chronic arguments often reactively over-focus on making counter-points to everything the partner is saying, or over-correcting.*

He says, "When I came home after supper…"

And she quickly steps in with, "It wasn't after supper, it was at least 8 or 9…"

If the debate isn't about when he got home, then why even go there? It just interferes with the normal progression of a conversation and makes the partner feel like they have to be overly accurate with everything they say, and that their partner is only looking to find fault.

While this may be an attempt to broaden his perspective, or an example of balance that's gotten out of control, we have to recognize that what we need to be trying to do is find common ground, or *points of agreement*, in order to move forward. The more we stay focused on differences, or petty inaccuracies, the further away from resolution we get.

---

**Rule #7. Own up to your contribution to the problem first, and it will open the door for your partner to examine his part.**

---

*Change typically starts with us.*

If a pattern of hurtful behavior exists in a relationship, each partner is a part of that pattern. We may not be the *cause* of that problem, but we often will do something that plays a part in helping or hindering it. We can even be doing the "right" thing to deal with it, but it's still the wrong choice for our particular partner.

Changing our own part is particularly effective in situations where the "problem" is occurring as a *reaction* to what we're doing or saying. If we change our approach, then, predictably, the reaction should change since our reactive partner's behavior is dependent on us. It may not get the desired reaction, but at least now we're approaching it by looking at what is in our control first.

Even if it is a character or personality issue in our partner that has occurred in past relationships, we still play a part in assisting with the solution. Even if it is just a *supportive* role, how we choose to be supportive can make a big difference. It is part of being a team rather than giving the rejecting message of "It's *your* problem; *you* deal with it."

If your partner is owning the problem but isolating himself ("It's *my* problem, *I'll* deal with it"), then he's also missing the opportunity to draw closer by exploring how his partner can help him overcome whatever his struggle may be.

If we have already wrestled through what we may be doing that has maintained, created, or worsened the problem, sharing our efforts with our partner can open him up to examining his own end. If he is able to see that we're not putting it all on him, that we are already recognizing that we play a part, we are sharing the burden of responsibility for the relationship from the very start. There is then no need to point the finger or pass judgment; it is a shared problem.

◆　◆　◆

Some couples get very hung up on apologizing – that to apologize is taking *all* of the blame and they're not going to do it. Again, they are operating by extremes – taking *all* of the blame or *none* of the blame. Why not just apologize for your *part* of the problem?

Some couples have to itemize what percentage of the problem was theirs – 45%, 83%...92.5%. This seems ridiculous but I see it frequently – couples who get so nit-picky about every little thing.

In working towards a strategy for resolution, it does become important to examine what each person's part of the problem is, but not for the purpose of assigning who is the most to blame. The purpose of examining each part is to give each side strategies that they can use to help fix the problem.

In the example of Peter and Patty, at the picnic Patty was trying to explore Peter's upset but he wasn't giving her much to go on. Patty *did* press Peter past the point that he asked her to let it be, but, on Patty's behalf, Peter really didn't do a good job in the moment of letting her know what was going on with him. Because he didn't fill in the blanks, she kept coming back for more information. He was denying his upset with her, but he *was* upset about being at the picnic. Peter was focused on Patty letting him be, rather than recognizing that he was giving off noticeable signals that a caring partner wouldn't ignore – he was acting withdrawn and moody at a social function.

What Patty could have done a better job at while at the picnic was expand on her reasons for being concerned about Peter. By focusing just on was he angry with *her*, he did answer her question by saying "no". Peter was being concrete, something that is stereotypically male. By her continuing to press the *same* concern repeatedly, it was like calling him a liar. What she needed to do was broaden her line of questioning regarding the possibilities of what was going on with him, or possibly share her observations of how he was coming across to others at the picnic to raise his awareness. Maybe those paths would have been more productive.

How Patty could approach it might be something like this:

Patty says, "Peter, when I see you withdraw like that I don't know what's going on. The only thing I know is to try to ask questions. You're saying I should just leave you be, and I understand needing space, but you're also telling me now that you *were* upset, just not with me. What could I do different in the future that wouldn't shut you down, but also get the information I need to be able to let it go?"

She's sharing with him her frustration at not being able to be more successful at being heard, and this is honest since part of her frustration is not just with him but with her own lack of success with this problem.

Up until this point, her way was to press him with questions until he became angry. His way was wanting her to let him alone without a decent explanation, which just distanced him from her. *Neither individual strategy worked for the relationship.*

By putting it on herself, what she could do differently, Patty's not pointing the finger at Peter, yet she's still pulling him into the resolution process.

Because she's remaining vulnerable, the odds stay good that he might start to own some things that he could have done differently. But even if Peter just provides some solutions for her part only, Patty doesn't have to back off. She can ask for more, but she needs to make sure she doesn't undo what she's already accomplished. So it could look something like this:

"Okay. I'll try to hang onto your suggestions. It's good to know there's something I can do to make it better. But I'd like to balance this out because the other part of this is what I need from you when this happens. Can I make some suggestions?"

Notice that she's not making any accusations. She's essentially thanking him for what he's offered, and then she's moving on to let him know that her needs have not yet been met. She doesn't start making demands; she asks him *can* she make some suggestions (Rule #19).

She's not assuming an overly submissive role by doing this. This is the same role I'd suggest for a male. She's giving him the benefit of the doubt and she's showing him respect by requesting his attention, asking for the opportunity to give some feedback. This is good manners, folks - the same way we'd hopefully treat our best friend!

If he cares about her needs, which most partners will say they do, he'll *invite* the suggestions. If he says he's not interested, and this is the pattern, then you've got some serious things to consider concerning the future of the relationship.

How well he listens may be a reflection on his listening skills and the priority he places on the relationship, but much of it also has to do with the *delivery* of those suggestions.

Granted, there are unhealthy individuals out there who would have no problem with letting everything be our fault, but what I am discussing here is a method we can use to defuse a potential conflict by validating an issue through ownership. The fact that we are acknowledging our own contribution to the problem validates our partner's perception that it's not a one-sided issue.

---

## Rule #8. Take turns talking and listening.

---

You say, "Well, of course, we're going to take turns". But remember what we already talked about - over a period of time in a relationship you naturally start to take shortcuts. Part of how we take shortcuts is that we no longer take the time to completely hear the other person out. We finish his sentences for him. We speak over him with our own point. We try to "cut to the chase". We motion him to move on with it instead of dragging things out. We're overly focused on thinking about our response before he's even halfway done with his. As a result, there are times when we don't give each other enough room to be heard.

If you look at the conversation between Peter and Patty, they weren't interrupting each other. They seemed to be taking turns. But neither was really *listening* to the other. Each was stuck in his own perspective.

Patty was focused on how Peter ruined the picnic. Peter was focused on how Patty kept pressing him even though he told her he wasn't angry with her, and how he could never get credit for his efforts. Both think they're addressing the problem, but they're only *explaining* their own issues. Each wants recognition of their particular perspective.

Each person is trying to work on the relationship, because they're still investing a lot of time in trying to talk it out. But they don't know how to stop what's going on because the only strategy they have is to *explain* – and so the conversation just goes round and round. This is a very typical scenario. It isn't that they are incompatible or that this relationship is doomed.

For many couples, in the early part of the dating process, you took the time to talk. You focused your attention on hearing each other out and responded rather than reacted to each other, giving the message that you, maybe more than anyone else, understood where the other was coming from. You weren't in any rush to get through the conversation. (Yes, I'm making assumptions about your dating life here.) But, now, you don't put that kind of energy and patience into it anymore and, as a result, you don't get the positive response you used to get.

If an argument is going nowhere, couples have to slow the discussion down to where one partner is saying his piece, and the other is taking time to understand it and validate it before the couple moves on. Because each is now feeling heard, they are able to move forward with the conversation. There is a heightened awareness of what has already been said, so there is not as much of a need for repetition.

◆　◆　◆

Take some time to look at the Listening Exercise at the back of the book (Appendix B). It walks you through a step-by-step interaction, teaching couples to re-learn how to take turns responding to each other and validating as you go. There are several reasons for this exercise.

- It often comes as a surprise to a couple just how difficult it has become to "take it slow" and take turns, and how much work goes into really focusing on hearing, clarifying and validating what the other person is saying rather than automatically turning the focus to you.

- It's often immediately rewarding if you or your partner have had little success in the past with feeling heard to discover that it is still within your ability to meet this need for each other. It's not some major leap of logic or perspective that is necessarily required to convince someone he has been heard and understood.

- It also helps you learn to separate the emotional reaction to what your partner is saying, since your focus is now outward, not inward. You are learning to view what your partner says as information, rather than continuing to look for any potential offense.

- For couples who are overwhelmed with the whole process of changing how they communicate, this exercise cuts things down into nice simple steps. It can be reserved for those times when there's been no progress because emotions are too involved, or the discussion has become too complicated.

For some people there is resistance to this exercise because they feel it overly structures a conversation into "baby steps". But by breaking a potentially emotionally-overwhelming conversation down into do-able chunks, we're able to walk through it relatively unscathed, without becoming distracted by side-issues or our own reactivity.

Do you always have to slow things down to this degree? No. But for the important things, and the issues that have a lot of emotional baggage attached, keep it in mind.

◆ ◆ ◆

For most arguments, there are two contradictions that we participate in that involve the extremes of under-listening and over-listening.

1. In terms of our partner, while we often are *under-listening* to the actual content of what he is trying to share, we tend to *over-listen* for the words he is using that contain potential offense.

2. In terms of ourselves, while we are often *over-focused* on explaining ourselves or our viewpoint, we are completely *under-focused* on the actual words that we're using (*how* we're expressing ourselves).

## Rule #9. Be respectful of your partner's perception of an issue. Don't define reality for the other.

*"Defining reality" is telling your partner how he thinks or feels.* It is not talking about how you yourself think or feel - it is making assumptions about your partner's thoughts and feelings and doesn't invite an actual conversation. It is a statement, not a question, so it doesn't leave room for debate, though it certainly creates a whole lot of debate as a result. Why should I even attempt trying to explain myself if you've already filled in all of the blanks for me and are unwilling to question your conclusions?

Patty starts defining reality for Peter when she says "I'll explain to him my concerns, but he thinks I should just get over it." Unless he has actually told her to "just get over it", which he denies, she is deciding for him that that is what he thinks. It would also explain why the discussion at the picnic became so problematic if her pattern was to chronically assume that he was angry with her, even though he was denying it.

Note that Patty made a statement a little later, saying that, "...I was *feeling* like Peter was in a bad mood." This is *not* defining reality for Peter. She's saying that that's how she felt, which allows that she might be wrong. It is, after all, a feeling, and we each have a right to how we feel.

Some people will say that this is just semantics, but it makes a major difference when we actively use this in conversation. To say "I *feel* like she doesn't care about me" versus "She doesn't care about me" is not saying the same thing. In the second version, I have already concluded that she doesn't care – how can that be argued if it's already been concluded? A decision has been made. But if I say "I feel like...", then there's room for debate since I'm allowing that that's just my perception. I haven't assumed the role of mind-reader.

Understand, I'm not saying it's okay to say something like "I *feel* like you're a jerk." While this may not be defining reality, it is still very much a *judgment*.

◆ ◆ ◆

A particular style of counseling that's often used by the media to make fun of the counseling profession is where the counselor spends a lot of time asking questions about how the client "feels". "Tell me how you *feel* about your dog dying." "How does it *feel* when he rejects you like that?" And, of course, the obvious answer is "I feel horrible! How do you think I feel?!"

When counselors *do* focus on clients talking about their feelings it's usually because the client is intellectualizing and detaching from his emotions, and so the counselor is trying to get the client back in touch with them. What I'm suggesting is that people use better terminology in their conflict resolution that doesn't *assume* what the other thinks or feels – how they go about doing it is up to them, I'm just pointing out one of the simplest methods.

A humorous misunderstanding occurred around this distinction when I was working with a couple in their second or third session.

The wife started off in a resentful tone with, "Well, Bob just feels that I should have two full-time jobs, a career and be a housewife all at the same time."

Bob's eyes are shooting daggers, teeth clenched, as he responds with, "That's not true! I only come off that way because she feels that a man is supposed to make all the money so she can go spend it!"

We'd already talked about not speaking for each other, so I stepped in to make a comment on their wording and each looked at me with a confused expression. I asked them what they didn't get and the husband replied, "I thought you said for us to talk about our feelings!"

They thought that because they were no longer telling each other what the other *thought*, but now telling each other how the other *felt*, that they were doing what I had suggested. What I had meant was for them to talk about their *own* feelings, not each other's. They were still continuing to define reality for each other and feeling just as upset by doing it.

◆　◆　◆

There was a simple experiment I was victim to in my high school psychology class. The class was just starting when, suddenly, a stranger walked into the class and "mugged" the student who was closest to the door. (Keep in mind this was back in the 70's when there was permission to do such "experiments". The whole event was planned and the mugged victim was in on it.) After it happened and the stranger ran out, everyone's jaws were hanging - either out of shock or not knowing what to do. The teacher came back into the room, having pretended to chase after the mugger, and started to interview the class on the details of what they'd seen. Every recount of what just happened was different – different accounts of what the mugger looked like, how he was dressed, even what had just happened – some more accurate than others.

It's important to remember that there are *two* people in a relationship. Even though we may be going through the same events, our experiences of those events and how we interpret them for ourselves are very different. *We cannot put ourselves in a position of saying that our interpretation of the event is the only right one – we can only say what our experience of the event was.* Especially in times of stress or strong emotion, our ability to interpret events accurately has greater likelihood of being impaired because we tend to only remember the pieces that are most relevant, or hurtful, for us.

This is why it is so problematic in a relationship when I elect myself as the only one who sees or understands things accurately. I do have the right to say what I did or didn't mean by something. I don't have the right to tell my partner what he did or didn't mean, think, or feel. By doing so I am saying that my viewpoint is the only one that matters in this relationship.

Part of understanding this rule is accepting that even my *own* perception is slightly removed from reality. My own history, insights and perceptions filter all information that comes into my brain from the outside world.

I am *not* saying to question your own judgment to the point that you can never take a stand on anything. I *am* saying we need to learn to give each other the "benefit of the doubt" - that we may be missing something that the other person sees, hears or understands that is important for us to consider in order to balance our picture.

◆　◆　◆

Let's talk briefly about how to best respond to an "I feel" statement, where your partner has been successful with wording things in a way that doesn't define your reality for you. She could have said "You don't care anymore", but, instead, she says "I feel like you don't care anymore". If you respond with a simple "That's not true. Of course I do", you may feel like you're correcting her perception but you've actually just *invalidated* how she feels. Bear with me a second.

Patty confronted Peter about being angry with her, which he simply denied ("That's not true."). By leaving it at this, Peter was unintentionally being invalidating. If he was paying attention, he should have moved into a better explanation of what *was* upsetting him. ("I'm not angry at you, I'm just having difficulty letting go of this horrendous work week.") That would have been validating for her that he was, in fact, upset - just not with her. Her *observation* that he was upset was accurate; it was her *assumption* that was wrong. As I said before, with validation you are often, in that moment, ignoring the points you disagree on, and just focusing on the ones that you can support.

If a perception or assumption is incorrect, you will still want to correct it at some point in the conversation. But the validating part is the time you take to explore *why* your partner has that perception, or made that assumption, and being respectful of it – even when you disagree with it.

# Rule #10. Be willing to be wrong.

Ownership is validating. But to apply ownership we have to be willing to admit when we're wrong.

Most of us have a lot of past baggage attached to the words "right" and "wrong". When accused of doing "wrong", we react with anger, resentment, bitterness, guilt, and anxiety – any number of very powerful feelings that often have only a little to do with the current situation. It's sometimes more about what being wrong means to us, rather than the actual wrong we may have just committed.

Pride, control and competition all play a part in being unwilling to admit fault. Some people, even though they can see that they're wrong, will still not give their partner the "satisfaction" of admitting so. Yet, if you are not able to accept responsibility, then why do you expect it of your partner?

A relationship should not be about competition. It's not about being better than the other person or always being in the right. That goes against the whole definition of a team - being partners. If you've accepted that you're both going to be "missing the mark" at different points in your relationship, then learning to admit wrong isn't about fear of judgment or attack – it's just owning up to your part of the problem in order to better the relationship.

◆　◆　◆

The person who is not afraid to admit his faults shows greater strength of character than the person who has to constantly hide or deny any shortcomings. How freeing to be able to say, "You know, you're right. That wasn't the best choice for me to make, and I can see how it could have hurt you." Suddenly, I've changed the whole battleground. It's no longer a battle because I'm not participating in the struggle. I've admitted to some fault in the situation. I've validated my partner's perception. And

I've remained humble in the process rather than turning things into a blame game.

Hopefully, I'm also setting the stage for my partner to own up to his own mistakes. As in a support group, where one person starts to admit to some personal issues, suddenly it's okay for everyone else to talk about faults in front of the rest of the group and to not feel judged.

By putting ourselves above blame, we automatically set ourselves above our partners. Granted, some mistakes are more detrimental to the relationship than others, particularly when they aren't "mistakes" at all but things done intentionally to hurt. But what I am referring to is the common ground you should be trying to create in your relationship where honesty is rewarded and being vulnerable is welcomed rather than rejected. You are admitting to what didn't work in order for things *to* work.

Sun Tzu's classic "The Art of War" was about military strategies for the fighting samurai. In it, the warrior who has to hide his weaknesses lives in fear of them being discovered and used against him. The man who has owned his vulnerabilities is at an advantage because he is hiding nothing. His weaknesses can't be used against him because he has already acknowledged their existence.

◆　◆　◆

Keep in mind what I said earlier about ownership. Being willing to be wrong and admit it is great, but sometimes resolution requires going past ownership and being willing to agree to new strategies if things are going to actually improve. Repeated ownership without meaningful change loses its value pretty quickly.

# Rule #11. It's okay to disagree.

Part of understanding validation is recognizing that you don't have to agree with your partner's perception in order to validate it. For people who need others to constantly be in agreement with them in order to feel at peace, agreeing to disagree can be tough.

There are *interest* differences. He likes sport shows and she likes home improvement shows. Each doesn't really care for the other's preference, but they can live with the difference so long as each interest is valued as being equal – one's not treated any more importantly than the other's.

There are differences around *routine* where she would prefer him to clean up the house to her standard, but ultimately has to accept that he's not her. Usually, in these situations the key is that the partner *is* accepting responsibility for getting the job done, but there is room for him to do it his way.

There are differences in *skills* or *personality type*, where he has to accept that what he is asking of his partner is an area that is a natural strength for him but not for her – where he may be naturally social but she is not. They still need to try to stretch to accommodate each other, being open to learning new skills, but expectations need to remain realistic - that he's not using himself as the standard of what is acceptable.

There are differences around *core beliefs*. If you're a Christian and your partner's Jewish, you need to be mindful that your job is *not* to convert him. Your influence is stronger when shown by your respect for his faith, not your judgment.

Peter could have agreed with Patty that he was upset. But he couldn't have agreed with her that he was upset with her when he wasn't. Her trying to force his agreement of something that was inaccurate, didn't work for either of them.

In seeking a resolution to the situation, in this particular situation, Peter and Patty needed to do more than just agree to disagree. If there was to be a better outcome, they would have to decide on better strategies to make things work. They were each holding out for the other to adopt their particular solution, and nobody was budging. They needed to be more realistic that the solution had to be something that would work for the relationship, and would probably require a small stretch for both. Patty needed to stop defining reality for Peter, and Peter needed to be more open to discussing Patty's concerns.

◆ ◆ ◆

Ultimately, in seeking resolution, learning to agree to disagree, to live with the things that aren't going to change, comes down to whether the issue is *need-related*. If these are core needs that are not being met (security, significance and fun), then you've got a problem.

There are couples who have stayed together because at least one spouse stopped looking to have core needs met by the partner and has coped by developing a life outside of the marriage – getting security and significance through friends, family, work, and his spiritual life. While some marriages can survive like this, more often the couple has learned to simply co-exist rather than having an intimate relationship.

If these are *preferences* that are not being met, then it's more a matter of learning to accept and live with it, recognizing that the more important needs *are* being satisfied. The message we often give to our partners by pushing our preferences, past the point of educating them about our likes and dislikes, is not only "You need to be more like me and less like you", but "There's something wrong with you for not being more like me".

I should add that if enough preferences go routinely unmet, at some point it may actually impact a need. But the solution isn't to require that each individual preference be met, rather to look at which are the most important, or which have the most impact on meeting the underlying need.

The biggest predictor for successful change in a relationship comes down to the couples' state of *readiness* to change. Those couples that are willing to do whatever it takes to have the relationship they both want, are more likely to be successful in creating it.

You won't get the relationship you want based on good intentions or desire. You have to act on it and live out that commitment to seeing it through. Part of it is being willing to die to self, your way of doing things, at least to a degree, for the sake of the relationship. Part of it is remaining open to learning and adopting better approaches. Part of it is taking forward steps, even if you're not completely feeling it – which is okay, because the feelings will often follow.

## Summary Points:

1.  Balance the negative with the positive. Just as it's easier to walk through a house and notice what needs to be done rather than what's already been done, it's important to stop and force ourselves to pay attention to what's still working. How can you positively motivate your partner to change only by complaining? When approaching your partner about an issue, try to think of a few positives to share first so he can see that you recognize there are good things happening too. If you are the first to identify the positive in your partner, it keeps him from feeling the need to defend himself.

2.  Own up to your contribution to the problem first, and it will open the door for the other to examine his part. This isn't suggesting that you assign percentages to how much was you and how much was him. And it isn't suggesting you admit your part and then demand that he admit to his. If I can focus on my end of any dilemma and approach a solution, I am inviting my partner to help me without ever pointing the finger.

3.  Take turns talking and listening. While this seems elementary, it is incredibly common that the longer you have known somebody the easier it is to take shortcuts with your communication. And

the most common experience in miscommunication is, "You're not getting it. You're not hearing what I'm trying to say."

4.  Be respectful of your partner's perception of an issue. Don't define reality for the other. If your partner feels a certain way, you can't tell him that he doesn't feel that way. No matter how old the relationship, you need to operate from a position of giving the other the "benefit of the doubt", being open to being educated about what they say they actually think or feel. Each of us has our own perceptions of an experience but reality is somewhere in the middle.

5.  Be willing to be wrong. The wise partner is able to recognize that admission of wrong can be a faster path to resolution than many others. It's not just remaining vulnerable; it's about accepting ownership for your part in a problem. If you are staying focused on maintaining an honest relationship, and are trying to create a safe place for both you and your partner, admitting wrong is an act of trust.

6.  It's okay to disagree. Some conflicts do not require resolution. It is unrealistic to expect that your partner must have the same opinions or agree with everything that you do.

## Discussion Questions:

1.  **Of the validation "rules", which ones do you have the most difficulty with?** Why?

2.  **How are you going to put the rules that are most often ignored on such a conscious level that they are actually being applied when issues are being discussed?**

# Chapter 5
# Processing the Issue

So you've already brought your issue to the table and you're working on providing mutual validation as you go. The next stage is called *processing* the issue, where you and your partner are taking the time to examine the issue from different sides in order to better understand each other's perception and insights into the problem.

While I addressed them in separate chapters, validation and processing are very much intertwined. As you and your partner discuss and explain, you're also validating as you go by continuing to respectfully hear each other out.

Jim and Janet have been married for fifteen years. During the first couple years of their marriage, things seemed to be going pretty well. When they started to have kids, however, the business of the day distracted them from continuing to attend to each other's needs and they slowly drifted apart - without even realizing what was happening. At the point that they have come in for counseling, they are both feeling very stressed and at a loss as to how to change direction.

In response to being asked why they are coming for counseling, Jim steps in first, saying, "We've gotten to the point where we've actually been talking about separating. Neither of us wants this to happen, but we can't seem to work anything out. Janet seems to get upset about the least little thing that I say and will blow up at me, and then I'll retreat. We're locked in a stalemate and keep going through the same routine."

Janet is tight-lipped while Jim is talking, nodding on occasion and looking very serious. They're sitting on the same couch but there's noticeable space between them. Janet's arms and legs are crossed tightly. Jim seems a bit more relaxed.

"Jim's right," she says. "It *has* gotten to the point where separation comes up. And he *does* run away from conflict. As far as my blowing up at the 'least little thing', I have a lot of stress on me and I feel like I'm not getting much help around the house – so, yes, I do 'blow up' at him."

Janet's tone is becoming more strained as she continues to speak. It's obvious she's fighting a desire to "blow up", even now.

Jim counters, "My job involves a lot of responsibility at this point. I can't manage the load I carry during the day without some of it coming home at night. Janet gets upset when I have to back out of helping with the kids sometimes because there's work to be done that can't wait."

Janet responds, now avoiding looking directly at Jim, "I work part-time on top of taking care of the home. I can't do it all! Sometimes I feel like he's just using his work as an excuse to not have to deal with the rest of us!"

"If that were the case I wouldn't be coming home at all. I'd stay at the office!" Jim is quick to reply. He's becoming more emotional, but there's more hurt in his voice than anger.

"You may as well stay at the office!" Janet shoots back. "I doubt the kids would even know you were gone!"

"Don't bring the kids into it!" he reacts; now the anger is coming. "I can't stand it when you try to use guilt to get me to give in. Stop trying to be my mother and manipulate me into doing what you want by using them!"

"Don't you dare compare me to your mother! I'm nothing like her!"

"I said you were *trying* to be my mother; I wasn't comparing. Besides, *she* doesn't have temper problems, so it wouldn't apply."

"Then why don't you marry someone more like her?"

Jim starts to say something and catches himself. He visibly steps back from the argument, withdrawing. He looks at me with a shrug. "You see," he says. "This is exactly what happens at home."

---

## Rule #12. Keep in mind the goal of the conversation.

---

It seems that one of the hardest things for couples to do when discussing an issue is to keep from getting side-tracked. It's so easy to bring up additional issues when trying to explain yourself. But when you do this, your partner automatically tries to address the extra issues and, before you know it, no one can remember how things got started. You've overwhelmed each other with so many different problems to be addressed that you're left with the feeling that if this much is going wrong there's no hope for the relationship. The initial topic goes unresolved and the issues continue to pile up.

Jim and Janet started off agreeing, for the most part, on why they were there for counseling, though each was focused on the other person's part of the problem. It didn't take long before the kids were brought into it, then Jim's mother, and things were getting pretty far off-track from where they started. The direction of the conversation was lost and so many other things were being added to the mix that it quickly became impossible to sort it all out or resolve everything that was being brought up in one sitting.

Once you've already identified to your partner what you're wanting (Rule #2), it's helpful during the ensuing conversation to be asking yourself "Is what I'm about to say going to help us move closer to a resolution or just complicate things?"

If it's a problem you're discussing and there's something that needs taken into account in order to better understand the situation, then it probably needs to be brought into the picture. Just be careful not to bring things into the conversation that are just going to add another layer of issues.

Sometimes there needs to be stopping points in the conversation if it's a complicated one. You need to ask if it's okay to move forward or if something else needs to be said. You need to give each other a breather if emotions are starting to get overly involved. You need to make sure you're still treating what's being said as information (rational logic) rather than just reacting (emotional logic).

If there is great difficulty in staying on task with the conversation, you might want to consider writing the initial issue down on a sheet of paper. Check it from time to time during the conversation to make sure you're sticking with the original topic.

When a side issue is brought up, ask your partner "Is that issue important enough that we need to address it as well?" Often times, if the other person really thinks about it, he will realize it really isn't something else he wanted to get into; it was just that the one issue set off others.

If something else is brought up that *is* important and needs to be discussed, write it down as well and come back to it *after* you've dealt with what's first on the list. The practice of staying focused like this helps with learning awareness of your *own* communication style and how you contribute to your own frustration by getting off the subject.

◆ ◆ ◆

Sometimes there is no resolution because the only "goal" was to vent. Now that one partner's essentially "burned the house down" with an emotional outburst, he's satisfied because he got the emotional release he sought – but at what cost?

*Venting only works if it's done with some degree of control.* If you strike out at anything and everything in your anger, saying things that are hurtful and have no purpose other than to wound, you're risking losing any respect your partner has for you – being viewed as a Child throwing a tantrum or an angry Parent trying to punish.

◆　◆　◆

Sometimes it is difficult to remain goal-focused because you are feeling so emotionally overwhelmed by the content that you can't adequately explain yourself or reason things through. At such a time, finding a resolution may not be possible but it doesn't mean you shouldn't approach your partner at all.

The goal in such a situation may be to simply educate your partner about what you're going through and maybe some of the reasons why, so that he doesn't misinterpret your behavior. Further, a goal may be to express to him what you need from him while you're going through whatever it is you're wrestling with, even if all you're asking for is some space to sort things out. That way he's not "in the dark" and having to resort to guesswork.

---

## Rule #13. Exercise loving accountability; avoid value judgments.

---

Value judgments are easy to make. In fact, they are *so* easy we often don't even notice when we are making one. A *value judgment* is when we are making a judgment about someone else's character – the kind of person we think he is.

Words that would commonly express such a judgment might be "lazy, slob, selfish, childish, evil, sick, perverted", etc. And, of course, the majority of curse words have all sorts of weighted judgments built into them if they're directed at us. We may not say these judgments out loud but, often, when we see another's negative behavior, we automatically attach a judgment to his actions.

Looking back at Janet and Jim, at the start of their conversation they did a fairly decent job of avoiding any *stated* value judgments. Usually, at this point in a relationship, however, even though the statements may not be *openly* stated, they are often being *implied*. For instance, Janet says "I feel like you're just using your work as an excuse to not have to deal with the rest of us". Jim may automatically interpret this in his head as, "She's saying I'm selfish and don't care about my own family." If Jim doesn't communicate his inner dialogue to Janet with a question ("So are you saying I'm selfish and don't care about any of you?"), then things can get heated pretty quickly without any surface reason for why offense is so intense.

When Jim accidentally mentions "mother", there are obviously all sorts of negative judgments that Janet has with this, though Jim stated none. But, you can't avoid every implied judgment. You can't control how your partner is going to read into everything you say. But you can work at clarifying his interpretation.

It's interesting to note that, at this point in Jim and Janet's relationship, when things *do* get close to character judgments, the couple retreats. They still have some sense of boundaries as to what's "going too far" and, when that line is about to be crossed, they back off – or at least Jim does. However, for some couples, the character attacks start before the third or fourth sentence is said.

It is difficult enough to work on issues when you are just focusing on specific behaviors that need changing, but when you take it to the level of a judgment, how can you work out compromises around that?

"She says I'm 'scum'. So what's to work out? Does she want to live with scum? If that's how she sees me, then why is she still here? And why should I want to stay?"

Judgments are not only an attack on the character of a person, they also undermine the core of the relationship which is supposed to be based on trust, acceptance and commitment. If I am making a negative judgment about my partner's values or character, *I am rejecting the person that he is*. That creates a dilemma for the relationship since how can I continue to have a relationship with you if I've just told you I don't even like who you are?

No relationship can handle character rejection for very long. When a relationship is no longer working well, it has to be able to fall back on the friendship to catch its breath, because the friendship still provides for some degree of acceptance. If the rejection runs that deep, to the point that there is no longer even a friendship, then the relationship is in dire straits.

◆ ◆ ◆

People tend to jump to conclusions and judge their partners based on *pieces* of information before they actually understand the *circumstances* behind what was said or done – often missing a vital piece of the picture. Take this court scenario:

- a man is in court for the shooting of a clerk in a department store
- witnesses testify they saw it happen
- the man accused of doing the shooting has admitted to it

On the surface, this sounds like an open-and-shut case. Are you already forming a judgment about this man and what might have happened? But let me add a few more facts first.

- the shooter has no criminal history
- the cashier is in the hospital but he'll live - the shot injured his shoulder but it will heal

- the shooting occurred in the sporting goods section of the department store

Is your picture changing yet? Okay, let's talk about the *circumstances*.

- The "shooter" was in the store looking at guns in the sporting goods section.
- The clerk was giving the man pointers on cleaning and loading a gun.
- The gun was not supposed to be loaded.
- The shooter was not intentionally aiming the gun at the clerk when it went off.
- The court hearing was around who was negligent in this situation.

Do you see the shifting that occurred in how you would naturally perceive this case based on simply the surface facts versus the circumstances? Often, when we judge our partner, we do not take the time to discover the circumstances around what's going on; we simply judge based on the surface information.

If he is acting upset towards us, do we take the time to explore what's going on first, or just jump to a quick conclusion that he is unfairly rejecting us and, therefore, "cruel, mean, evil"? There are countless possibilities as to our partner's motives, but we tend to reach out and draw a quick conclusion. If we do that often enough, over time, the message that we are giving is that we automatically assume the worst about him - that we don't trust him - that we don't give him the benefit of the doubt. And then he starts to form his own judgments of us for our quick assumptions of him.

◆ ◆ ◆

In addressing each other's mistakes, we all need to learn the best paths to exercising loving accountability. Some partners will respond to *any* criticism of their behavior as depriving them of their freedom because they feel that demands are being made of them. Others view accountability as simply being responsible to the relationship, and an opportunity to demonstrate the strength of their love by respecting the partners' request for change.

Many times we get a negative response from our partners when we are approaching accountability because we are doing it in an overly punishing or judgmental way. We may even be using the right words, but our tone and expression can be conveying many other contradictory messages that aren't being said.

There are two terms I want to use that will shed better light on the distinctions I'm trying to make between being accountable and being judgmental. *Conviction* is when my accuser (whether it be myself, circumstances, or someone else) is pointing out my mistakes in such a way that I am able to hear it, respond to it, and be motivated to make the necessary changes so that the mistake will not continue to occur. Conviction is a *positive* thing because it *inspires* change. If I feel convicted of something in a relationship, then *I'm* the one who has accepted my own guilt at having done something that's harmful. And *the response to a feeling of conviction is a desire to correct the error – setting the wrong to right.*

*Condemnation* is when my accuser (whether myself, circumstances, or an individual) is pointing out my mistakes in such a way that I am overwhelmed with feelings of judgment or rejection. Even if the accusation is accurate, it is being done or I am reacting to it in such a way as to be overwhelmed or pushed away. While I may be able to hear it and, even on some level, recognize the truth of it, it is unlikely that I will know how to respond to it because of all the emotions it is setting off in me. I am being presented such a negative picture of myself that it is doubtful that my motivation will be in a positive direction for change. In some individuals, where condemnation has become a regular part of their lives, ultimately they come to accept themselves as "bad" people, and, as a result, lose any motivation to try to do better.

Try to think in terms of conviction as being equivalent to *accountability*, and condemnation as equivalent to being *judgmental*.

Accountability is a part of any healthy relationship where a commitment to respecting the relationship has been made. When things are happening that are a threat to the relationship's present or future, accountability comes into play. If my partner, knowingly or unknowingly, is doing something that is harming the foundation of trust or respect of the relationship, I am responsibly accepting my part of the relationship by approaching him about it, just as I would hope he would do the same with me. I need to do this in a way that conveys respect and love, even if it's damaged respect and love, separating the sin from the sinner.

Accountability is also where I or my partner have promised to do something and failed to follow through on it. We are gently reminding each other of the commitments that we have made.

Holding someone accountable is usually done by:

- focusing on the problem *choices* and *behaviors*, not the person's character
- staying focused on expressing the unmet needs, not giving in to anger or attempting to punish
- keeping a calm, neutral or loving tone
- being specific and not using over-generalizations (example: "always/ never")
- finding strategies and solutions for change, which also include any way *you* can assist the change
- attaining a commitment and specific plan for follow through
- sharing the dilemma that's created when they fail to follow through
- if your approach has a negative impact, asking them for direction in what approach would work better (understanding that the issue *does* still need to be addressed)

If you have difficulty knowing the difference between accountability and judging in how you communicate, ask for feedback.

"How do I come across to you when I have an issue? Do you feel like I judge you?"

"How do you prefer that I approach you in terms of accountability?"

"How can I talk to you about this without shutting you down?"

"If how I'm approaching you is pushing you away, how can I approach you in a way that doesn't, yet also addresses my concern?"

You don't have to have all the answers up-front, or know the magic words. Accountability is applied by both partners, so it is a mutual struggle to find the best approach. What works best for you, might not work well for your partner.

---

## Rule #14. Approach the conversation with options, not ultimatums.

---

Making judgments automatically sets the stage for *ultimatums* to occur, but I strongly suggest you *don't use ultimatums unless you're ready to act on them.* If someone continually threatens to leave a relationship but keeps backing down and staying, ultimately he loses any respect from his partner because of the false threats and seeming attempts at manipulation. If you're not really going to go, then you shouldn't make the threat in the first place - there's better ways of letting your partner know you're upset.

You may be trying to attach a priority to the issue for your partner, letting him know that it's a deal-breaker for the relationship if the problem continues, but you should be trying to deliver this as information, not a threat.

I know very few people who respond well to ultimatums because it comes off as an attempt to control without compromise, and has a degree of rejection automatically built into it. Even if the ultimatum creates compliance in the partner for a time, resentment usually begins to grow in the background and, eventually, rises to the surface.

By staying with options and potential solutions, we are keeping our partners focused on their *freedom and choice*. Ultimatums are about *forcing* a choice.

When Janet starts to react with, "Why don't you marry someone more like her", she's getting close to an ultimatum. The fact that separation has been brought up in the past indicates that possibly there have been ultimatums used before. Both are focused on the dilemma for themselves, rather than options to make the difficult realities easier, even if that means just accepting the fact that the workload at present is very stressful for both of them.

◆　◆　◆

At the same time, for some issues there is no compromise and an ultimatum *is* required. These are the situations where the behavior is either self-destructive or destructive to the relationship to the degree that there can be no further toleration. For instance, I am not suggesting that you compromise around such a thing as an affair. I've seen some relationships where the "compromise" for someone staying in the marriage was that, unbelievably, a spouse got to keep his mistress on the side. This was incredibly degrading to his partner and an insult to the marriage. Such a situation would call for an ultimatum – choose the mistress or choose the marriage, but you can't have both.

In that kind of situation, the concern wouldn't be about the spouse resenting having to acquiesce to his partner's demands; it would be the partner resenting her spouse for putting her in a position where it was even necessary for her to make the demand.

## Rule #15. Try to treat emotionally-weighted words as information rather than attacks.

In the same way that being too emotionally distant can be a problem in a relationship, it can also be a problem to be so close that we've now fallen "under the radar" - so close we're no longer seen clearly. We need to be emotionally available to our partners, but we also need to keep enough perspective that we don't take everything too personally. If friends disappoint us, we may be hurt but we can often move past it because of any number of reasons:

- it might have been a mistake
- we know they care
- they have so many other good qualities
- it was an isolated event
- it's their issue, not ours

We can separate that event or statement that was hurtful because our relationship boundaries are intact, our filters in place.[5]

In a love relationship, where we have supposedly made ourselves vulnerable to this other person, we are automatically more sensitive to any signs of rejection. We can't minimize that they wouldn't have done or said such a thing if they knew who we really were because, supposedly, they *do* know. So we have to turn to other defenses – most of them being rather primitive. If I'm being rejected, then I reject back! So there!

For those who are too emotionally *close* to a problem, they need to gain enough emotional distance from the problem so that they can get a better perspective on it.

---

[5] For people who have poor boundaries or fragile self-esteem, almost everything becomes personal. Even something that a stranger did or said to them is difficult to separate from who they are – "What is it about me that made them say that? Why do they not like me?"

For those who are emotionally too *distant*, they need to learn how to lower their emotional walls, and empathize more effectively. (For the purposes of Rule #15, we're going to be focusing on emotionally distancing yourself from the problem in order to gain perspective.)

◆　◆　◆

In terms of visual imagery, consider the simple image of water rolling off of a duck's back. Ducks' feathers secrete a type of oil that prevents water from soaking in, so instead it rolls off. The negative words that your partner occasionally aims at you are the dirty water and your job is to let it roll right over and off of you rather than to let it sink in - staying focused on what's going on *beyond* all those words.

Reactive words are only the surface layer and can often be very misleading from the actual hurt going on underneath. Your concern is with what's *creating* those words, and how to get to it, *not what's actually being said.*

If I can recognize that my partner's being reactive, or that I must have just stepped on one of his emotional wounds[6], then it should be easier for me to not take whatever happens personally because I understand that, at that point, it's no longer really about me. It's the wound talking; or maybe the wounded child striking back. I need to accept that when someone gets that upset they don't mean half of what they actually say.

Your image doesn't have to be a duck. It can be whatever represents the same thing to you – an island, a calm pool, an armored tank, whatever. The idea is to choose something that is protected but not so closed off that you are no longer connected to the conversation. Then your personal gauge becomes, "Am I still this calm pool or am I allowing myself to get stirred up?"

If you're getting stirred up, then you need to focus on whatever you need to do to calm yourself down. If you *can't* get calmed down then you don't need to be participating in the conversation any further. Take a healthy exit - excuse yourself or let your partner know that you're too upset to try to get any further with the issue at the moment.

---

6　　Harville Hendrix "Getting the Love You Want", "Keeping the Love You Find".

◆　◆　◆

*We don't get upset by events, or what people do or say to us. We get upset because of what we tell ourselves about those things.*

Jim coming home late is a neutral event – just a fact. Janet doesn't get upset about Jim coming home late – she gets upset because of the things she tells herself about him coming home late. She makes the mental leap from "He's late again" to "I can't stand it when he does that" to "Once again his job's more important than us" to "I don't know how much longer I can put up with this".

While we can't altogether "shut off" our self-talk – we *can* work on replacing it with statements that are not so disastrous or destructive. Again, we have to become aware first of what our self-talk says.

I'm not suggesting you lie to yourself by trying to pretend that something's okay when it's not. But, in situations where the emotion is outweighing the actual event, you need to be able to talk yourself through it. Just as when your partner's reaction is over-the-top, your internal questions to you need to be, "Where's this coming from?", "Is this possibly a misunderstanding?", "Why is this bothering me (or him) so much?"

By asking ourselves questions that help us think things through, we're applying the same logic to why we ask our partners questions - to move them to thinking rather than lost in their emotion.

If our heads are full of thought distortions fueled by our emotional logic, we have to be able to doubt our own conclusions knowing that we tend to gravitate towards distortions when we're upset. You need to have some reality-based thoughts that effectively counter your own distortions to help keep you grounded.

◆　◆　◆

The majority of emotional arguments in a relationship revolve around loss of perspective. As a counselor, what I am constantly doing is trying to help move couples back to a larger perspective of what's going on with them in the moment. That larger picture restores a sense of control over what's going on, and gives the couple a better sense of what they need to do to make it work – having stepped back from the intensity of the situation, they can start to see other options than just continuing to react.

Ideally, the couple is learning to hold up those healthy mirrors to each other *before* things get lost in reactivity.

# Rule #16. Remain vulnerable.

Being willing to be wrong is about being able to acknowledge *fault*. Being willing to be *vulnerable* refers to a general *attitude* towards your partner.

It goes against our nature to put ourselves in situations where we know pain is a likelihood. Our own instinct for survival wants to protect ourselves from possible pain and death. Yet, the only way that we can have a relationship where we have achieved the closeness that we desire is to be willing to show our flaws and trust that our partner will respect that confidence, knowing there will be times when ideals aren't met.

Because we are all initially children in relationships, it takes time to learn how to respect each others' flaws. In school, flaws are usually made fun of by our peers, so we hide them. As adults, we have learned to put on different fronts of "having it all together" both to impress and to protect us from criticism. But, ultimately, we cannot hold a double standard, demanding honesty and vulnerability from our partners yet being unwilling to give it in return.

Men, especially, aren't raised to be vulnerable. Traditionally, they are raised to be independent – to make it on their own in the world. That initial independent image, not advertising weaknesses, is supposed to be an advertisement of strength. There's pressure to be that almost-perfect person if you're going to succeed in business, life and relationships. The fear is that if we acknowledge our faults, or needs, we will be rejected or judged, taken advantage of or attacked, or simply seen as being weak.

The dating world further promotes this need to put out such an attractive image as bait if you're going to be successful in catching the perfect man or woman. So just how long can you maintain that perfect persona? Sooner or later, if someone's in your life long enough, he's going to see through the cracks anyway. Are you just going to pretend that the cracks don't exist?

So we already have a problem with letting people see our needs, flaws or weaknesses. But *the defenses that we use to survive in the world around us will actually stand in the way of an emotionally intimate relationship if we use them at home.* We have to re-define our definitions of weakness and strength. To let down those emotional walls with our partner takes strength. To be vulnerable with our partner takes courage. To show our hurt and tears is an act of trust. To admit fault and a need for personal improvement is being willing to model true Adult behavior. To express our need is acknowledging to our partner that there are things we rely on him for, part of what makes him feel significant. These are all things that need to be supported and rewarded when they occur.

Even in the animal world, where instinct is very much a natural part, there are models for what I would suggest. Let me call on all the dog lovers out there. Have you ever seen two dogs fighting? It may be play-fighting or not. The dogs will growl at each other, bark, maybe pace around each other looking for an opening. Often, they're trying to establish dominance - which makes it completely surprising that, at some point, in the middle of this struggle, one of the dogs will inevitably roll over on its back, exposing its most vulnerable areas - the throat and belly! Why would it do that? It knows it's being attacked, yet it's intentionally making itself vulnerable to be hurt.

Well, if you continue to watch, the next odd thing that will usually happen is that the attacking dog will start to back off! It doesn't go for the jugular when it so easily could. Why? Because, *by being vulnerable, the prostrate dog has established that it is not a threat.*

Now, I'm not saying that we're animals. I'm not calling you a dog. I'm not saying that you should roll over on your back in the middle of an argument (though that can defuse things pretty quickly). I'm trying to point out the simple fact that being vulnerable removes you from the position of being perceived as the enemy. And *it sets an example for your partner and the relationship that you're willing to risk.*

Not only are you changing the attack mode of the conversation, you're putting it on a different level – a much more mature one. While it is often the *weaker* animal in nature that rolls over, with humans it's usually the person who has more emotional discipline that is able to do so.

By being vulnerable you aren't acknowledging your partner's dominance over you. He hasn't "won" anything. You're showing the greater insight and self-control by being able to defuse the situation by stepping out of the fight.

Now, when that dog first rolled over, the dog left standing may still keep barking for awhile. It may feint and bluff to see if the dog will stay on its back or start to attack again. It may not automatically just assume that the threat is gone. If you suddenly move to a position of vulnerability in your conversation, your partner may not initially trust that. He may suspect a manipulation, or a trap. He may try to test it. But if you remain consistent and can maintain that stance, you'll prove your sincerity.

What will often happen in arguments when one person attempts to remain vulnerable, if the partner does not initially respect this and continues to attack, then the vulnerable one will give up their vulnerable stance and jump back into attack mode as well. *Our choosing to remain vulnerable cannot be dependent on our partner's willingness to be vulnerable in return.*

It is important to note that all dogs are not alike, and there *are* some sick puppies out there. There are those dogs that are cruel at heart that will go in for the kill. And there are people out there that will take advantage of your vulnerability and step all over it. But that's useful information too. If this is a pattern, it potentially tells you something about your partner's character - that they are willing to continue to attack someone who has chosen to be defenseless.

We need to examine how we, intentionally or unintentionally, sabotage the vulnerability that we desire from each other. To remain open enough to say "I don't know the answer...," "I'm afraid that...", or "I need..." can invite undeserved criticism or ridicule. Because we are often brought up to value strength and despise weakness, we often step on perceived acts of weakness in our partners when they, in reality, may have been taking a step of faith in being vulnerable with us by sharing something very personal.

In the example with Jim and Janet, both were sharing valuable information about their perspectives and needs – both had good points to make about the realities of their situation. The job situation itself was a valid problem – the job *did* make heavy demands on Jim, and Janet was also feeling overworked. It was a difficult situation. The problem didn't have to be one of selfish motivations on either side; both were putting a lot of work into maintaining the home through maintaining their jobs. It didn't have to be turned into a battleground by attributing the causes of the problem to selfish motivations.

◆ ◆ ◆

We need to have the freedom in relationships to take turns with being "needy". Some people cringe at the very word. When I use that word I don't mean being an emotional leech that clings and smothers. Being able to express your needs in a relationship is being willing to expose at least a small degree of dependency to your partner – you *do* need acceptance, to feel valued, loved and trusted, and you do need help to make the relationship work. If you cannot humble yourself in order to express these needs, chances are, if they're not being met, they're not going to be met.

The word "humble" is appropriate since often our avoidance of being vulnerable, aside from our instinct at self-protection, has to do with *pride*. Pride can say, "I'm not the one who's in the wrong here", or "I don't need any help". Yet there's great validity in the proverb "Pride comes before the fall." Pride stands in the way of a relationship. It makes compromise extremely difficult. Pride pushes us into a rigid position, at a time when flexibility is what's needed most.

My frustration with much of couple's counseling is that people often don't come for help until it's almost too late, often due to their pride – like the stereotypical male who won't stop and ask for directions until he's utterly lost. On occasion I will meet incredibly wise and fore-sighted people who recognize that things are moving in a dangerous direction and they want to prevent a possible crisis by seeking help now rather than later. It's so much easier to intervene at that stage rather than when things have gotten so emotionally entangled that the only way to achieve safety and perspective is through physical distance.

◆　◆　◆

Being vulnerable is a two-way street. It's us being willing to be vulnerable with our partners, and welcoming them to do the same with us. It would obviously be unfair to share our fears, concerns, and needs with our partners, yet be rejecting of them when they attempt to do the same. Also, it would unbalance the relationship to welcome our partners' disclosures, yet never open up and trust them with anything personal of ourselves.

---

# Rule #17. Don't negatively compare your partner to others.

---

Often during arguments there will be this temptation to compare a partner to someone who is modeling better behavior - be it friend, family or foe. Yet, long-standing relationships with friends and relatives have been undermined this way, though that was not typically the motive for the initial comparison. Whatever the intention, making comparisons gives the impression that you are looking at somebody else more desirably than your own partner, which is a problem for the relationship, especially if this is a pattern. Even if you are in the habit of drawing positive comparisons to others, it still hints that you are using others as a gauge for your approval of your partner.

Jim wasn't making comparisons, but Janet automatically heard one when he brought up her acting like his mother. He didn't literally mean *his* mother; he was referring to her attempt at parenting him through the use of guilt. This might have indicated a deeper insecurity on Janet's part, being sensitive to comparisons, or maybe Jim's mother had been an issue for them in the past.

Of course, you're put in a bind if your partner *asks* you for comparisons – "Honey, am I like that?" While this may be a simple opportunity for a compliment, assurance or education, now it's possibly catering to their habit of comparing. And it's a potential trap in the same way as "Honey, do I look fat in this?" is.

If you know your partner well enough that you know they are simply seeking information and can use the honest feedback in a helpful way, then this might not be a problem. But if their self-esteem is poor and they are constantly feeling "less than" through their comparisons, then it's probably not helpful to participate in the comparison game. You can still provide assurance or be complimentary without having to cooperate with continued comparisons.

---

## Rule #18. "Never" and "always" need to be stricken from the couple's vocabulary.

---

The words "never" and "always" fall into the category of "black-and-white thinking" or "all-or-nothing thinking". They are extremes.

"You *never* help me clean up around here."

"You *always* have to have the last word."

Well, sorry, but, for a relationship, there is no such thing as those two words.

It may feel to you like it's never or always. But it is likely that now and then there is the occasional success. You may feel that, in comparison, the desired behavior hardly ever happens, but you're not allowing credit for it when it does. And when a relationship's at the point where everything is focused around things going wrong, giving credit for what's going right becomes vitally important.

Better to put things in terms of "I appreciate the times where you have gone out of your way to help, but I still need more of a consistent effort with cleaning things up." It goes back to Rule #6 ("Balance the negative with the positive"). If your partner is feeling like they have been "helping clean things up", but not in a way that is significant to you, you may need to better define what you mean by "cleaning things up". It may be a simple matter of two different definitions that is confusing things, and if they had a more exact idea of what you meant you might see better results.

Using "never" and "always" in an argument comes off as a blatant exaggeration. It puts you in an extreme light for using that terminology – that you're blind to your partner's attempts to help or change. It also undermines the partner's motivation if he feels he doesn't get any recognition for the times he *has* tried.

We're not just trying to be careful to use more accurate words in our conversations, but also in our own minds. Even though I may not be saying "always" and "never" openly to my partner, if my *internal* dialogue is constantly hanging onto those distortions, then I'm still viewing the situation unfairly.

Jim and Janet's conversation didn't involve "always" and "never". There was still enough conscious control that words like "I feel like", allowing for personal perspective, and "sometimes", a healthy qualifier, were still being used. But you could also see how it was getting close to Janet feeling like Jim was at the office "*all* of the time", and her having to handle "*all* of the work" at home.

You may feel that minding your wording is a petty thing, but it can make a very big difference. You may say, "He knows I don't really mean always or never." But I've rarely seen a couple that was so laid-back that there wasn't an underlying negative impact from the regular use of those words.

---

## Rule #19. Make requests, not demands.

---

Personal boundaries, what keeps me able to see my partner as separate and "other" from me, deteriorate with familiarity, and in times of stress the filters we use to monitor our own behavior are likely to get dropped. In such times, it's important that you don't forget the simple methods for showing respect to your partner. If you want respect, you need to show respect, and one of the simplest ways of doing this is through making requests, not demands.

Since it wouldn't be healthy to be the Parent dictating over your partner, or the Child making pouty demands, you're trying to maintain an attitude of freedom and choice in the relationship, rather than turning it into being all about obligation, responsibility and a long list of "to-do's". You're *asking* him for compliance with certain things, trusting that if he cares, he is taking your request into account. *It doesn't mean that if he loves you, he'll do everything you ask.*

It also doesn't mean that you assume he heard you the first time and is ignoring your request, if you're not seeing results. There's no harm in following up a request with seeking further information, or providing a reminder. And there's no harm in doing some problem-solving with your partner if there are things that are getting in the way of satisfying that request.

Jim and Janet's conversation didn't offer any solutions, so it was unclear if "requests versus demands" was a problem for them. The only demand of note was Janet forbidding Jim to compare her to his mother, which she could have done in the form of a request. ("Jim, I'd really appreciate it if you didn't bring your mother into this, or make those kinds of comparisons.")

The obvious dilemma that comes with making requests is when the request is understood but still being refused. At that point it comes back to is this a preference for you, or a need? If it's a preference, you may simply have to learn to let this particular request go if there's no compromise that can be worked out. If it's a core need, then accountability comes into play, and the partner needs to be approached in a considerate way that directly addresses his accountability to the relationship.

Especially when trying to work out resolutions to issues, there's fine wording involved in trying to avoid being demanding. "I need more help around the home", even though said as a statement rather than a request, accurately identifies the need without coming across as "You'd better start helping more", which is a threat.

Ideally, you are working toward phrasing things in terms of questions, "Could you please find more time to help me out around the house?" This may sound painfully nice, but it is also choosing to address your partner with humility and respect, something you're wanting in return. You may feel their behavior doesn't deserve either, but to put things on a demand level before it has really reached a point where accountability needs to be brought into it, is choosing to turn things into a hostile power struggle.

Some people will automatically feel like they have the right to make demands because this is, after all, *their* partner. But even just saying it in those terms makes it obvious that they are looking at their partner in terms of property, which they aren't. This is another, separate human being with feelings, thoughts, needs and desires of their own. They aren't yours to order around. They are yours to express your needs to, but not yours to control.

---

While couples often work hard to keep the relationship from getting to a crisis point, sometimes they need to embrace it rather than run from it. The discomfort of a crisis often gives us the motivation to make the necessary changes. Avoiding getting to a crisis delays that change. If you can be pro-active and do something to reduce any need for that crisis to ever occur, that's wonderful. But for those who just live in toleration and misery rather than approach change, a crisis is usually what has to occur to get things moving again.

Keep in mind that the problems of the relationship tend to expose the weaknesses of each individual in the relationship - the things they need to get better at. The positive piece of any crisis is that, if the relationship is to improve, it will usually mean that *each* person in the relationship changes in a *necessary* way.

## Summary Points:

1. Keep in mind the goal of the conversation. Is what you're about to say relevant to the current issue? Will it help clear or muddy the water? Is it to the benefit of the relationship or harmful? Discuss one issue at a time. Avoid counter-issues or becoming side-tracked. You may have to write the issue down in order to stay on track.

2. Exercise loving accountability while avoiding value judgments. Try to separate the act from the individual – avoiding words that are a judgment of someone's character (lazy, jerk, slob, tightwad, stupid, etc.).

3. Approach the conversation with options, not ultimatums. Ultimatums are often inappropriately used as a form of control or manipulation. If you haven't already discussed options for *possible* solutions, go there first. Don't issue ultimatums unless you are prepared to act on them.

4. Try to treat emotionally-weighted words as *information* rather than attacks. In a conversation that contains sensitive personal content, try to focus on how this information can be used to gain better understanding. If the words are ones spoken in anger, try to move past your partner's surface communication, focusing on the overall content not the upsetting detail.

5. Remain vulnerable. It is more important to talk from our vulnerable pain than from our anger. Vulnerability is less likely to draw an attack since it is an act of kindness, not vengeance. If you are open to admitting your *own* shortcomings, it can encourage your partner to examine his, without becoming defensive.

6. Don't negatively compare your partner to others. Be careful of drawing comparisons too frequently, either positive or negative, between your partner and others. It indicates that you are using others as a gauge of your approval for your partner.

7. "Never" and "always" need to be stricken from the couple's vocabulary. There is no such thing as a behavior happening never or always. Using these words in an argument comes off as a blatant exaggeration and doesn't allow for those times when the negative behavior wasn't occurring, or when the positive was. It also puts the partner in a position of feeling like, "Why should I try?" if they are not getting any recognition for the times when they have tried.

8. Make requests, not demands. This is your partner, and you need to show respect if you want respect. Since you're not in charge of the relationship, it's not a good idea to assume that role with your partner by telling him what he "has" to do. If you want to keep things on the level of choice, be sure to term things as requests.

## Discussion Questions:

1. **Of the processing "rules", which ones do you have the most difficulty with?** Why?

2. **How are you going to put the rules that are most often ignored on such a conscious level that they are actually being applied when issues are being discussed?**

# Chapter 6
# Resolving the Issue

You will often find couples who have gotten really good at stating their *opinions* about a problem. They both recognize that, yes, there *is* a problem. They may even agree on what the problem is. But both have different ideas of what the solution should be. So the problem persists because each is caught up in his own solution and neither is willing or knows how to budge from that position without compromising what he believes should be done.

The final stage of conflict resolution is actually *resolving* the issue, if validation wasn't enough. This is where you and your partner are taking the time to arrive at a solution, or possible solutions, that best meet both sides' needs.

Often when people are looking for solutions, they are trying to identify "the one right answer" to the problem. Well, in the same way that there is usually not just one thing that caused the problem, there is usually more than one solution.

The initial act of seeking resolution strategies is brain-storming *possible* solutions. People can get so overwhelmed with trying to seek for something deep and immediately impacting, when the initial part of the process of brain-storming is just getting into problem-solving mode. *Any* possibilities at the start, no matter how ridiculous, are at least getting the process rolling.

A sense of humor, if not distracting from the goal, is almost always helpful in keeping a perspective while seeking an answer.

The solutions that don't work might need to be tossed aside, but sometimes they may just need to be fine-tuned. Sometimes they didn't work before because they weren't tried for long enough, or weren't attempted consistently.

**Nancy and Nate had been married for about 7 years. The first two years of their marriage seemed to go pretty well while riding on the momentum of their infatuation for each other. During the fourth year, Nate had had a brief "fling" with a girl from work who is now no longer working with his agency. Several people from his office had gone to a workshop in a neighboring city and had spent the night. Apparently Nate and the girl in question had been drinking and things went too far. Nate had confessed the one-night affair to Nancy. They had separated for a month and then got back together, neither wanting to lose the relationship over one foolish night. There had been no further infidelities. They talk about having kids but wisely want to work through their current issues before bringing children into the picture. Neither relates their current issues as involving the affair.**

**They've been in counseling for a couple sessions and are at the point where they're trying to work out actual strategies to put their relationship back in balance since both feel things have gotten off track.**

**Nancy is explaining the current impasse. She is very matter-of-fact. "We've been taking the time to sit down at least once a week and that seems to be helping to keep things from getting overwhelming, but we're having problems with agreeing on specific solutions.**

**"You'd suggested we start putting some priority on spending more time together just having fun, rather than talking about the problems all the time. So we started to talk about the things that we could do together and, while we came up with a couple things, there wasn't anything on the list that we both liked to do."**

"Nancy's really into her craft stuff, and I'm not," said Nate, joining in. "I like to watch my sports games or actually go see a game, and she could care less. We used to go to games back when we were dating but I guess she just went because I wanted to."

Nancy nods. "That's true. I really don't have the patience for that kind of thing anymore. We made a list of movies that are out, but we couldn't find one we both liked. He likes action and comedy, while I like dramas and romance. We both like movies, we have that in common, but not the same ones."

"So we didn't get anywhere on that one this week," added Nate.

---

**Rule #20. Some of the best solutions are the old ones – in seeking solutions don't try to re-invent the wheel.**

---

One of the easiest ways to find possible solutions for the present is to think back on your past history as a couple and identify those things that you have done in the past in similar situations that worked. Often, couples were doing positive things during the dating period because the relationship took priority and there were fewer distractions. Or the marriage had some initial golden years before falling into a routine. Now that the focus has drifted to other demands, the couple has stopped doing those positive things. So now they need to think back and pull some of those activities or habits back into the present. And it can simply start with the question, "What did we used to do? When we had more success with this, what was it that we were doing different?"

The current issue may not be relevant to any prior history, but the starting place is always to go back to old successes first, for guidance in the present.

Nancy and Nate's history was being labeled as out-dated. They had come to a point where neither was interested in the things that they used to do, at least not in continuing to do them together. What had changed was that they were no longer doing things simply because the other person was doing them – it was now about how interested they themselves were with the activity. But does that mean you should *only* do things together that are just as much fun for both? Ideally, it would be nice if those activities existed. But you need to be careful that the relationship isn't gradually becoming about self, rather than "us" - which leads to the room-mate relationship. If healthy love continues to be a motivator for the relationship, then sometimes a shared activity is done just because it's shared – for example, how some couples will find fun ways to share in getting the chores done, or a home project. The chore or the project itself is secondary.

What Nate and Nancy needed to bring back from the past was engaging in mutual activities just for the sake of being present with the other - having fun not because of what they were doing, but because they were doing it together.

◆　◆　◆

Solutions don't have to be restricted to the history of your current relationship. Other prior relationships provide keys to success as well, even relationships that you weren't in yourself but witnessed in others.

The important part here is to be very careful about making continuous comparisons (Rule #17). Sometimes one person will have had a fairly healthy childhood and he keeps using that as the model for the relationship. However, the partner has come to where she has started to resent the other's parents, because they are constantly being used as the example of what to do. While they may actually be a good model, over-using them as a verbal reference has created a sore spot. It would be better for further suggestions to not include the source.

You also have to be careful that you not use any one relationship as the sole template that dictates the way your relationship should be. Your relationship is *your* relationship, not anyone else's. It needs to be a combination of what works for both of you, and not an exact replication of somebody else's life.

Especially if you are looking at prior romantic relationships, it is *not* suggested you keep telling your partner "Well, my ex and I used to do this, and that really seemed to work..." You don't want to be giving an unspoken message that another romantic relationship was better than your current one.

This is just using discretion, being tactful with what you say – attaching a healthy filter. It's the same kind of filter you use when you're editing your anger, still expressing the hurt but weeding out what would be destructive.

---

**Rule #21. If you have already given some thought to possible solutions before you "come to the table" with the issue, it will move the process more quickly to a solution.**

---

Many people were raised in families where feelings were vented the majority of the time, and no solutions ever came out of it. The kids from these families grow up thinking that how you deal with your feelings is to call them as they see them, regardless of the outcome. Yet if you want to see a positive result from the issues you raise, you need to put more thought into solutions.

Rule #7 suggested you consider your part of the problem first before discussing an issue. Rule #21 is the follow-up to this, with thinking through *possible solutions* ahead of time. It assumes you've already decided that you're looking for more than just an apology, or a listening ear, and you need some actual changes made.

You might think that because you're coming with solutions *before* the discussion that this rule should be under "identifying the problem". However, you still will often need to go through the steps of identifying, validating, and discussing the issue, before you start to unload the options you've thought of.

Thinking of it in terms of the strategies that are used in business, typically, most bosses are not inspired to change after being given a list of the things that are wrong with how they manage things. They are usually much more responsive to suggestions on how things can be improved when it is obvious that the changes will benefit the company. While a couple is not a business, they are both based around relationships. And, usually, real people are more open to a solution-focused approach than problem-oriented.

◆ ◆ ◆

While it is fine to voice your *preferences* for a particular solution, the idea in approaching resolution is not coming into it with "the" solution where it's simply a matter of you dictating what's going to happen. Your solutions are *suggestions* to be discussed, examined and worked through. Your partner may have some solutions of his own.

If none of the solutions are good enough, you don't just give up and walk away. You take one or two of the ones that have the most promise and fine-tune them until you have something that may be a bit of a sacrifice for both, but will ultimately meet each other's needs.

In Nancy and Nate's case, they may have actually spent the time thinking about what to do together prior to discussing it. Their mistake was not in preparation, but with their focus - they focused on what *wouldn't* work rather than on what *would*. In other words, they continued to focus on the differences. They should have been focused on finding common ground, and, if none could be found, creating it.

## Rule #22. Solutions should be tolerable to both sides, not an imbalance of one side constantly "giving in". Try to avoid black-and-white solutions.

Rule #22 has already been stated in many ways in the content of prior rules; however, it also needs to stand on its own. You are trying to avoid developing a pattern in the relationship where one person is usually getting his way and it is creating resentment in the other. You are also trying to avoid thinking in terms of "his way/her way" since this leads to control struggles.

Nancy and Nate were stuck in thinking of "his way/her way". They couldn't yet think in terms of finding the middle ground where they were sacrificing a little and getting something back. There were the things he wanted to do and the things she wanted to do, and neither showed much interest in the other. And so, the resolution process stopped short with nothing accomplished except for a greater awareness of how far they'd grown apart.

If you are rolling your eyes and saying an exasperated "Fine!" when you agree to something, you probably have not reached a satisfactory resolution. Often couples will give in for the sake of avoiding a hassle but just as much damage can be created in the long run by those who constantly take a backseat in the relationship. They may be doing it out of not wanting to create more conflict or because what their partner wants is more important to them than what they want, but, ultimately, if this is an ongoing pattern, they are allowing another's will to absorb their own and they will come to regret it.

You may be a passive person but the relationship needs *your* voice just as much as your partner's if it is to retain a shared identity.

◆　◆　◆

The most common solutions come down to:

1) *Let whoever has the greatest need in the situation, or the greatest competence, assume responsibility for that particular thing.* For example, someone who wants the clothes folded a particular way becomes responsible for folding the clothes. Or, whoever is the best cook assumes responsibility for the meals.

For those people who have a particular way of doing *everything*, however, this can create a dilemma since obviously they can't assume responsibility for everything. They will have to prioritize and assume responsibility for the things most important to them, and be willing to let the things that fall to the partner be completed in a way that falls slightly short of mirroring their own.

Ideally, the partner who is less "particular" will still give an effort that stretches a little beyond his comfort zone in trying to reach his partner's standards, but it needs to be accepted that the goal of every task is not to perfectly meet that higher standard.

2) *Agree to a compromise, where the standard is set somewhere between the particular expectations.* You want to go shopping for three or four hours while he only wants to go for one, so you agree to two hours if you're going to go together. Or you agree to balance the places you're going to go to so that each person is getting to go to places they're interested in. Or he only accompanies you for an hour or two, and you do the rest on your own.

One person wants to work on the yard, while the other wants to go to a matinee. So the movie-goer helps out with the yard work to make it possible for both to catch an early movie.

3) *Agree to disagree.* Some issues are not important enough to have to work through to a compromise. Sometimes we get caught up in petty arguments simply because we have the need to be "right", or have our way, and don't let up until someone gives us that recognition or we drive them away. Recognize that it's unrealistic to expect that your partner's opinion has to reflect your own.

It would be unrealistic to expect that your partner should accompany you every time you went to a movie. Or that every time you do yard work, your partner should be there to help. It's okay to do things separately as well as together. The problem is always with the extremes, when *everything* has to be done together, or *everything* is done separately. Or when *everything* has to be done a certain way.

"Agree to disagree" usually comes down to whether the issue is a preference or a need. Preferences don't require agreement. Needs typically require some type of action or some degree of change.

4) *Try both ways.* If it's a his/her impasse, sometimes a nice work-around is to take a few weeks doing it his way, then a few weeks doing it her way and afterwards, with the new information of what it was actually like doing it both ways, they can sometimes have a better discussion and both agree on one particular path.

---

## Rule #23. To forgive does not mean to forget.

---

We've all heard the phrase "forgive and forget". When I hear this I automatically think of the counter – "He who forgets the past is doomed to repeat it". If we forget the mistakes we, or others, have made, we lose the opportunity to learn from them. And we typically set ourselves up to repeat them.

If we are in denial about a problem, pretending that it doesn't exist, then we will not be taking steps to avoid the problem - as we would if we were owning up to it.

In relationships, while it is vital that forgiveness occurs, forgetting is not a part of that process. This does not mean that you badger or punish your partner about the past, or hold a grudge against him. It is quite possible to forgive while not forgetting, and yet not be ruled by the negative feelings associated with the memory.

Part of forgiving is learning to exercise grace in relationships, knowing that in the same way your partner has issues, faults and imperfections, that you too have your own collection.

People will often learn to forgive through learning empathy for the offender. We can see how there was a misunderstanding. We can see how the circumstances of the day were affecting his behavior or thinking. We are able to see how that person's past has led him to be who he is. We can understand the negative influences on his life that may have twisted or damaged his heart. He had a series of bad relationships. He never learned how to share his feelings. And so, through this empathy, we can learn to let go of the pain that that person caused, because we've come to understand it better – we've "normalized" it.

However, *sometimes forgiveness means letting go of something that was wrong no matter which way you view it* - which is very hard to do, but still necessary.

We automatically seem to expect justice or fairness even though our experience in life may be that we seldom get it. If we have been done a wrong it seems only natural that someone should be punished for it. Yet real life says that wrongs occur on a daily basis and that they often go unaddressed or with punishments that don't come close to fitting the crime. Yet, *if we don't let go of it, at some point the issue becomes our own because the anger that is attached to the wrong begins hurting us, rather than the wrong-doer.* And that anger enters other areas of our lives, feeding into bitterness and negativity. If we don't at some point find ways of exorcising it from our minds and hearts, it will become poisonous to our physical and emotional health as well as to our relationships.

In the situation with Nate and Nancy, you couldn't help but wonder if there was not still some underlying hostility at work because of the affair. It had only been three years ago, and, just because it was no longer discussed or labeled as an issue, did not mean it had actually been resolved. Neither was openly hostile towards the other in sessions. There was a lack of the subtle put-downs and cuts that often continue to go on as back-handed methods of payback. But you had to wonder why there seemed to be this lack of desire or motivation to arrive at specific plans of action. Each had done a good job of establishing his own interests; but the relationship had grown apart. Eventually, if the resistance or procrastination continued, they would have to start exploring the reasons for that resistance and find out if forgiveness was still an issue.

◆　◆　◆

It is very difficult to let go of something when we never get the apology that we desire, or the acknowledgment of guilt or fault. If I have learned that a person has wronged me and is unrepentant about it, then I have potentially learned something about that person's character, and I have some decisions to make based on the following:

- How serious is the wrong?
- If it is truly serious is this someone that I am willing to keep in my life, knowing that the wrong is likely to re-occur if he sees no problem with his actions?
- If this is someone that I can't, or won't, remove from my life, how am I going to learn to deal with this, knowing what I know about him? How am I going to adjust my expectations of him for the future? How am I going to adjust the things I am willing to trust him with?

Relationships are based on *degrees* of trust. It's not as simple as "we trust" or "we don't trust". We learn over time who we can trust with what. So when someone routinely fails us in a particular area, our experience tells us this person is not as safe as we thought. That doesn't mean that he's not safe with *anything*, but it does mean he's not safe in that *specific* way that he proved untrustworthy. It doesn't necessarily mean that we have to totally cut this person out of our lives, but it does mean we need to be realistic about how much we extend our trust again.

On the other hand, people will many times avoid forgiveness thinking that if they do forgive they will have to allow this person back into their life, even though they know he's not "safe".[7] But forgiveness does not always mean reconciliation. You can forgive, letting go of the anger, while still respecting the new boundaries that you've drawn between you and him.

---

[7]   Henry Cloud & John Townsend's "Safe People".

When it's our partner that has failed us, regaining trust is often based on consistent evidence of change. But whether there is change or not, the core of the need for forgiving still comes back to what it does to *us* if we don't.

If our partner is unrepentant and essentially refuses accountability for his actions, we still have to weigh out how grievous the wrong is. If it's something he is unwilling to change, yet the behavior is that destructive, to us or the relationship, it brings the future of the relationship into question.

If I have been wronged and my partner *is* repentant, and takes consistent steps to not repeat it, then if I still refuse to forgive him, at some point *I* am now the one working against the relationship.

Yet, you can't *demand* forgiveness of another. And you shouldn't say you forgive someone before you're really ready to.

Sometimes forgiveness is a lengthy process that requires letting go of your hurt more than once. Events, conversations, or people will stir the memory of what happened before, and in that moment you may have that old pain overwhelm you again, and have to once again go through the process of letting go. But once you've let go the first time, the path becomes a little more familiar when you have to walk it again.

You have to be realistic that a painful memory will retain its pain – it leaves a scar. When you think back on it and still feel pain, it does not mean that you haven't forgiven. Forgiveness is better measured by whether or not you've been able to move on.

◆　◆　◆

Forgiving does *not* mean an absence of consequences. Yet we need to understand the distinction between *punishment* versus *consequences.*

Having an affair is going to have an impact on the trust of the relationship. Just because we're working towards forgiveness does not mean that the trust is automatically restored. One of the *consequences* of an affair is that the trust will never quite be the same as it was before. There will be continuing doubts and questions. The hurt that has been caused will need to be voiced. It is inevitable that we will need visible accountability, ownership, remorse and assurances in order to regain trust - even past the point that we've forgiven. These things aren't done to hurt, but are what's necessary to heal.

*Punishment* is usually focused on intentional harm or attaching a negative cost in order to reduce the likelihood of an event re-occurring. For the affair example, punishment would be the victim engaging in continued insults, threats and other destructive behavior towards the offender - trying to share the pain and maybe engage in payback of some type. Punishment is an easy indicator of a lack of forgiveness.

For some, the reason why they engage in punishment is that they feel if the partner doesn't experience visible emotional or physical pain, that the consequences won't be real enough for him, and so the problem will continue to occur. But we are trying to step away from parenting our partner, and move them toward a more Adult role where accountability still applies, but we are no longer engaging in methods that result in even more problems for the relationship.

---

**Rule #24. Try to resolve issues as they occur. However, each person should also retain the right to put off discussing an issue (not indefinitely) until they feel they can handle their part responsibly.**

---

The longer anger or resentment festers, the greater the damage to the relationship. It's that simple. Ideally, it is best to try to resolve your issues when they happen so that they do not accumulate.

Mental health is all about how people do or don't handle their emotional pain. We can't allow our degree of discomfort to decide whether or not we try to work something out.

Whether or not we approach an issue often has to do with the expectations we attach to the likelihood of our success in resolving it. If you haven't had a lot of practice with addressing issues, you need to be realistic that you will need practice. The fact of the matter is that you may not be successful in resolving things the first or the second time out (or maybe even the eighth or the ninth), but, hopefully, from each failed attempt you're learning more about what doesn't work and getting a clearer picture of what does.

◆　◆　◆

If it is not possible to resolve an issue within the day that it happens, then at least call a truce with a commitment to re-approach later on.

Sometimes just learning *how* to shelve an issue and set aside those feelings temporarily is a skill in itself. The temptation is to continue to throw a verbal barb out here or there, or use your upset with your partner to keep you from doing anything kind or loving until the issue is resolved to your satisfaction. But mis-managing the situation this way can end up creating a new set of issues. What you are trying to learn how to do is set boundaries between an issue that is on-hold and everything that is not a part of that issue.

If the relationship is a healthy one, then both a friendship *and* a romantic relationship should exist. This is where the unconditional regard of the friendship comes into play. The romantic relationship may be stressed by the issue at hand, but you should still be able to exercise respect for your partner by stepping back to the "friend" boundary that should still be intact.

The situation with Nate and Nancy was not an openly hostile one. If there was any anger there it was well hidden. They seemed more than willing to shelve the idea of dating for another week. Neither was pressing the issue. If anything, it would have been desirable if there were *more* passion there, which might have inspired them to be more aggressive in pinning down options for a night out.

There are situations that *do* require time for the best resolutions to occur. Some people are not good with quick responses or solutions and need time to sort things out – whether it's to figure out what's really going on with themselves, what a fair solution might be, or even just how to accurately express their own perspective.

Just be sure that the issues aren't put off indefinitely. A few days at most should be enough so that putting things off does not become a recurring tactic to avoid issues. If your partner can see that by giving you the room to cool down, or think things through, he is more likely to get a better outcome, he'll be more patient next time.

For those that insist on an immediate audience upon demand, despite an awareness that their partner's not at a point of readiness, and where it isn't a situation of avoiding the issue, forcing the issue rarely provides a best-fit solution. Instead, it becomes about control and immediate gratification at the possible cost of your partner's respect.

---

## Rule #25. Decisions made from strong emotion are not going to be good decisions.

---

People often have difficulty distinguishing between what is an emotional thought versus rational thought. Thoughts such as "I can't stand this anymore," "I hate him," "This is impossible," are based in *emotional logic*. They feel like clear thoughts that are directly connected to the situation, but what they actually do is fuel the fire for whatever feelings of upset are already stirring, clouding the issues.

Emotional logic can be either positive or negative. The emotional thought can be just as much "I love her" and still have little root in reality because the person may be experiencing infatuation. The point is that *the stronger the emotion the further removed from reality our judgment can become.*

Part of what makes being human so enjoyable is the range of possible emotions we can experience. Emotions are what add a level of quality or depth to our lives that would not be there were we solely rational individuals. But *while feelings can be useful guides, they tend to be poor decision makers.* (Sorry, all you romantics out there.)

Think of the people who got married a day, a week or a month after they met. Think of those folks who have a major blow-out and they instantly separate – only to get back together when the dust settles. *In the moment,* the decisions made seemed like the right choice, but, when time passed, it became obvious that the thinking was not clear at all and rash choices had been made.

I know that much of what we hear in books and movies is to "trust your feelings" and "go with what your heart tells you", but, frankly, I have heard very few success stories in relationships based on this philosophy. There are times where "going with your heart" works, such as a life direction for a career. But when such a philosophy is used in relationships, affairs occur, divorces, quickie weddings, becoming sexually involved before you're emotionally ready, and the list goes on.

One way of telling if you are being led by your feelings is if your conclusions go back and forth, since feelings change from day to day, moment to moment. This is why people who make most of their decisions based on their feelings typically have chaotic lives.

*The core of being "conflicted" is usually the struggle between what we rationally know versus what our feelings are telling us.*

◆　◆　◆

At the same time, reason is not automatically above error. Common sense is not found in equal proportions between humans and neither is the ability to think logically. What may seem logical to me may be some incredible leap of irrationality to the next person.

With Nate and Nancy, the feelings were calmed down, but to an extreme. It may have seemed quite rational to them to just ignore what had happened with the affair and try to move forward, not realizing the long-term effect such a strategy would have on the relationship.

The affair itself was an example of making a stupid choice based on momentary impulses with the assistance of alcohol. The fact that alcohol was present did not erase Nate's responsibility in the matter. He should not have allowed the situation to develop as far as it did. The emotional consequences of the situation resulted in a one-month separation where each gathered some emotional perspective on the situation and decided that the relationship was worth hanging onto, despite what had happened. But a lack of passion was now evident in their relationship. Maybe there was an unspoken fear that if passion was allowed to come to the surface again, negative feelings might come out as well.

That is why it is so important that, especially when we are considering making big decisions - whether it is regarding our work, our relationships, or our lives in general - that we seek wise counsel and don't rely solely on our own judgment. Like the hermit who has lived on the island for years by himself, his perception of the real world may be incredibly skewed because he has only his inner world from which to form his judgments.

◆　◆　◆

Emotion is usually based on the small picture of what I want most in this moment, without much regard for further down the road, or a very distorted projection of the future.

Reason is usually able to take into account the bigger picture of what's going to happen to my future if I do this today.

On occasion, in couple's work I'll hear a client say, "I'm done," in regards to the relationship. In that moment, he has gotten to the point where he's emotionally overwhelmed. He's exhausted. He doesn't feel like he has any energy left to continue trying to work on things. So, in that moment, if you forced him to make a decision about the future of "us", he'd say that, yes, he was done.

The partner who's lost in the emotional moment says, "So you're done? It's over? Just like that? How could you?! You quitter! After all I've done for you. I'm getting an attorney. I want you out of the house!"

The big picture voice of reason says, "Wait a minute. That's just how he feels *today*. In this hour. In this moment. That doesn't mean he's going to feel the same way in the morning. He needs to have some room, some time, to feel what he's feeling without being forced to make any decisions, just to be able to move through the emotion and see where things are when the emotional dust settles down." It recognizes that what we feel in the moment is colored by the emotion of the moment, and we can't afford to treat each other's emotions as the total truth of what's going on, just a partial truth.

Some people experience "emotional waves", whether the emotion is anger, anxiety, depression or happiness. If that emotional wave is a negative one, the partner will often try to fight the wave when it hits, or control the wave, or react to the wave, rather than recognizing that it's just a wave, and letting it pass. He takes that wave very personally, and treats what is said during that wave as cold hard truth rather than just the passing wave that it is. He fails to recognize that his partner's "type" is one that has waves.

While we need to take each other's emotions seriously, we also need to recognize that emotions come and go, that we do and say stupid things in the heat of the moment. If we're exercising grace, then there's room for emotional upset, while we wait out each other's feelings in order to get back to a place of reason.

Ideally, what is said in those moments of emotional recklessness doesn't cross the line of being completely inappropriate, or a deal-breaker for the relationship, or now it's no longer an issue of "letting the wave pass", now it's a matter of accountability that needs to be addressed.

## Rule #26. Be sure the solution is clear to both sides and specific enough that it can be immediately applied.

If a couple is successful in acknowledging a problem, accepting responsibility for it, and committing to doing better on it, they are still only partway there, because they are still operating only on intention. If there are no specific strategies in place, change often does not occur.

With two-part solutions, not only does each person have something to work on, there is continued loving accountability in terms of how each side touches base with the other regarding how they're doing. By giving continuing positive feedback and fine-tuning the implemented strategies, the couple stays on top of the issue.

For many couples, this is where they learn how to be positive in supporting change with each other, recognizing the small successes, rather than overly criticizing how things may still be falling short.

Couples need to have the discussion, "How can I best help you maintain your end of this change?"

◆　◆　◆

Sometimes it is fine for one person to assume responsibility and say "I'll take care of it" or "It won't happen again" and then you wait and see if the problem re-occurs. If it does re-occur, this is a good indicator that it's time for a more specific, and maybe joint, solution.

Let's take Nate and Nancy's situation a step further. Let's say that they actually agree on a particular activity together. So Friday night comes around and they know what they agreed on doing, but nothing has actually been planned. They meet a dead-end because no reservations were made, no one actually chose the particular restaurant or movie - already the evening's half over…and so they default and do nothing for that night. Again. All because of a failure to be more specific about who is going to do what.

People don't want to be bothered with the details, but there's a cost for ignoring them. It may seem like overly tedious work to plan things to such an extent; however, if your history is that it doesn't happen otherwise, then you need to take the time to plan.

---

Congratulations! You've gotten through each of the four areas for conflict resolution: identifying the problem, validating the problem, discussing the problem, and resolving the problem. If you made the effort to read through each of the sections, you should have some food for thought and, hopefully, some new tools to use the next time you approach a potential conflict.

Much of this may seem like common sense, but for many it may seem overwhelming. Keep in mind, this isn't about having to remember everything I've written, or do everything I've said - it's about starting to improve in whatever small ways that you can. The point of identifying so many different options is to give you any number of ways and choices to approach issues with better tools.

For those who may look at all of this as too much work, nobody ever said relationships were easy. And if you want the benefit of the rewards that come from being a healthy couple, it's completely worth it. Luckily, most of the work is on the front end. The more you master healthy resolution styles *now*, later on the tools becomes second nature.

If this is going to have any lasting impact on your life you will need to review these tools on occasion. It's one thing to know what they are; it's another to be focused enough on them in your discussions that you actually *apply* them. That's why there's a short version of the "rules list" included in this book (Appendix A) to use as a prompter when you're preparing to approach an issue.

At the start, you may need to look at the rules list in advance; then check yourself after you've made an attempt at resolution. You probably need to focus only on the tools that you continue to struggle with the most.

Invite your partner to assess which ones you still need work with. Your errors may be so natural to you that you don't even notice them when you're doing it.

*If you have a video camera, it can be very helpful to tape yourselves working things out and then go back and critique it, noting both what went well and what needs improvement.* It allows you to examine your own body language, facial expressions, vocal tone, and overall resolution style. Seeing yourself from a distance like this, having a mirror held up to your own behavior, helps create a perspective impossible to gain any other way.

In terms of rules versus guidelines, for those who need rules, because without them they'll be ignored, you might want to consider treating the 26 points I've itemized in these last four chapters as rules. For those looking for pointers to enhance an already functional relationship, treat these as guidelines that help keep you on the right road. The reward for using them is the greater likelihood of having a relationship unhampered by faulty communication and poor problem-solving skills. If you really want a healthier relationship and a happier you, there's your motivation for doing the work.

## Summary Points:

1. Some of the best solutions are the old ones – in seeking solutions don't try to re-invent the wheel. We often discover that old strategies worked for the relationship in the past but we just stopped using them. Since they're not completely new ways of doing things, it will be easier to adopt them because there's already a certain familiarity. We can also learn from other relationship histories – their successful strategies.

2. If you have already given some thought to possible solutions before you "come to the table" with the issue, it will move the process

more quickly to a solution. It's easy to bring up an issue in order to focus on how unfair or inappropriate an event or behavior was – a means of punishing. However, it's more helpful to approach an issue focused on options. Don't go into the discussion with *the* solution, but, rather, *possible* solutions.

3.  Solutions should be tolerable to both sides, not a recurring imbalance of one side "giving in". Try to avoid black-and-white solutions. A true compromise is the result of trying to find the middle ground where the needs of *both* are being addressed. Try to avoid two-dimensional thinking in attempting resolution since it operates in extremes (his way/her way, right/wrong, never/always) and usually implies a judgment.

4.  To forgive does not mean to forget. To forgive someone for a wrong act means to accept (not agree or condone) what has occurred and move on, letting go of the emotional baggage that is attached. However, it is not advisable to forget an event since, "He who forgets the past is doomed to repeat it". Once an act has been forgiven, it is not appropriate to bring it up to assist an attack or re-create an issue. Forgiveness does not mean an absence of consequences. We forgive in order to free ourselves from the consequences of un-forgiveness.

5.  Try to resolve issues as they occur. However, each person should retain the right to put off an argument until he feels he can handle his part responsibly. The longer anger or resentment festers, the greater the damage to the relationship. If it is not possible to resolve an issue before going to bed, then, at least, call a truce with a commitment to re-approach later. In order not to say something hurtful out of anger, it is better to give yourself time to calm down and think things through. Issues, however, should *not* be put off indefinitely.

6.  Decisions made from strong emotion are not going to be good decisions. When you are having strong emotions your thinking is no longer clear. You may *feel* like you are still thinking, but it is your emotions that are guiding your thoughts, not your intellect. Feelings change from day to day. Reason is more stable and a better foundation from which to make clear decisions.

7. Be sure "the solution" is clear to both sides and specific enough that it can be immediately applied. People have a tendency to speak in general terms when reaching a solution; they don't define the specifics and so the exact expectations for each person are not often laid out. If a specific plan is made, it is much more likely that both sides will comply because the expectations have been clarified.

## Discussion Questions:

1. **Of the resolution "rules", which ones do you have the most difficulty with?** Why?

2. **How are you going to put the rules that are most often ignored on such a conscious level that they are actually being applied when issues are being discussed?**

# Chapter 7
# Making and Maintaining Changes

For relationships that have existed for a while, negative patterns can create their own special kind of "rut" for the couple. Think of it in terms of the ox cart that has gone down the same path time and again, making a deep groove in the dirt road that the wheels automatically fall into. When you're trying to create a new path for the relationship, the hardest transition occurs during the initial efforts to step out of that well-worn "rut". But, with consistency and persistence, a new and healthier path can be created that also becomes routine in time.

The overall process involves: 1) recognizing the need to change, 2) deciding specifically what changes are going to take place, 3) making those changes and then 4) maintaining them.

## Initial Change

Dr. Phil's "So how is that working for you?" goes back a lot longer than Dr. Phil's TV career. "Reality therapy" is an approach historically associated with William Glasser, and Glasser's control theory. The focus is on taking conscious control of your personal choices. In a nutshell, "If it isn't working, stop doing it!" That *isn't* to say that, if the relationship isn't working, get out of it. It means take a look at what *you're* doing in the relationship that's not working and change the pattern.

Having done parenting counseling for years, parents would come in and talk to me about how their constant lectures to their teens did not seem to change the teen's behavior, yet it never occurred to them to stop lecturing and try something else. They were more focused on the teens changing their behavior than they were on their own – and feeling out of control as a result.

If you know something doesn't work, and you've tried it again and again, why do you keep doing it? Common sense would say that you should try a different approach. But, for many people, they stay with one approach because one is all that they know.

Some people will say, "Well, I'm *already* doing the right thing! You want me to start doing it wrong?" But there is more than one "right way" to fixing a relationship problem. *You may be doing what you were taught to do, or what makes the most sense to you to do, but that doesn't make it the most effective choice for the person you're in relationship with.* Why be so narrow as to say "Well, I tried this and it didn't work so I'm giving up." (Though, actually, "giving up" can be a positive change in the pattern as well. I've known relationships where when one person finally got to the point of giving up on trying to "convert" the partner to his way of doing things, they finally started to get along.)

It's relatively common to have someone come in for counseling who feels trapped in his career. He may have to hang on to his job because of financial responsibilities, family obligation, whatever. But he feels stuck because he feels that he has no choice but to stay with something he doesn't like.

The beginning work with such individuals is to help them see how they are making choices simply by staying with their job. They *could* leave. They *could* take something else for less. But they don't because they *choose* to do the responsible thing and continue to work where they are. And they fail to give themselves credit for making those difficult choices.

When people can come to see that they *do* have choices, even though those choices may not be pleasant, they start to feel a renewed sense of freedom. They aren't staying because they're stuck. They're staying because they're trying to be responsible. They're staying because their personal standards say they need to stay. They're staying because it's the best scenario of the ones available. And, sometimes, when somebody is put back in touch with the choices, he can think of other options that he hadn't considered before that would relieve some of the stress. Because he's no longer so emotionally overwhelmed, he can see beyond his present circumstances.

It's the same in relationships. When you turn the focus back on you and the choices you're making, rather than how you're stuck because of what your partner does or doesn't do, you're able to see that you do have options.

◆　◆　◆

With any new tools, it takes time to make an impact. Sometimes results are immediate, but sometimes things are more gradual. You've developed your patterns of acting and reacting for years, and it will take time to change those habits. People will sabotage themselves by trying something new and, if things don't change immediately, they give up on it. Patience is one of the keys to making change.

Often, if you try something new, such as controlling your temper, your partner will not initially respond favorably because at first the change goes unnoticed, or maybe he is suspicious of this new behavior. So we have to be persistent in staying the new course.

◆　◆　◆

*No one has control of you unless you give it to him.* If someone is trying to "push my buttons", I have a choice as to whether or not I'm going to let them. If you say, "There's no way I *can't* react when he says that…", then you're right. You *will* continue to react! But it's only because you choose to buy into that belief. You have to create doubt in your own conclusions. You have to entertain the idea that "No, I've *got* a choice here. I can continue to hand over control, which is not working, or I can let go of what's being thrown at me. I don't *have* to react. I don't *have* to let this get to me. I don't like it when it does get to me. How much nicer to be beyond letting this have its way with me."

There's an important concept that overlaps this called "*locus of control*".

I did a men's group a couple of years ago that was very memorable to me. In this particular group there was a very successful businessman and another man about 10 years older who had great difficulty holding down any kind of a job for more than a year or two. One of the striking things about this group was how they were very accepting of each other's station in life. They would confront each other but do it in a very gentle, non-judgmental manner. Over time, the businessman and the other man became good friends.

After several weeks into the group, the successful businessman spoke up. He addressed his friend who couldn't keep a job saying, "You know, I've been trying to figure out what it is about the two of us that has led us down separate roads. When I hear what you have to say I can relate to it and, in fact, we really seem a lot alike. But I think I've finally figured out what the key difference is."

The businessman continued. "You talked about how, when you first took this job you're in now, you put so much energy into doing everything just right. You took a lot of pride in how much energy you put into getting everything in a row, thinking up new ways of making it that much better than what had been asked, going over and above. But then you talked about getting disenchanted and feeling that you were thinking of quitting after a couple of weeks because you noticed that nobody else put the same effort into it - that they just 'got by' and didn't seem to care. And that it didn't seem to make a difference to your employers, either. You got some praise, but no raise. And *that's* the difference between you and me."

There was silence and then the other man asked "*What's* the difference?"

The businessman continued, "The difference is that I've never really cared what others thought about my work. *I* knew I did good work and that was enough for me. In time, the people that mattered noticed that I did a great job and I started to get the promotions. But whatever situation I was in, my motivation always came from inside me, not from the people around me. With what you've said, it seems like you've always let others decide for you what quality of work you did based on the recognition or lack of recognition they gave you. And so you always lose your motivation, because people never give you enough."

The businessman was right. The man who had left many jobs had an *external* "locus of control". His happiness was based on what was happening around him – his success depended on everyone else. The person with the *internal* "locus of control" was motivated by his own standards within.

If we are *internally*-motivated and in a relationship with a reactive partner, we are more likely to continue to be loving, *despite* his reactivity, because we stay focused on being consistent with the person we believe we should be. Easier said than done, yes, but in doing this, we also retain our self-respect and the offender, over time, is left with the weight of his/her own actions.

People who are *externally*-motivated often respond to perceived mistreatment by mistreating others in return, sometimes even mistreating themselves, because they allow those things outside of them to dictate what they should do. They lose, in part, because they are adopting the very behavior that they resented.

◆　◆　◆

Think of the relationship as a pond (don't laugh). Everything you throw into that pond has a ripple effect on the rest of it.

At one point in time that pond might have been a pretty attractive pond. It had a certain sparkle to it. You could see clearly into it. It might have had some pretty impressive fish swimming around in it. At one point in time, it was a peaceful place, somewhere you felt at home. And the pond improved over time because of how you tended to it.

But now the pond has gotten all stirred up either because of things that have been thrown into it (attacks on the relationship), something that was buried that's been dug up (the history you bring with you), or even because of nasty weather (life circumstances). You can no longer see into that pond because too much is happening, keeping its waters muddied and churning. You may *think* you know what's in that pond at this point because of your past familiarity with it, but you're having to make some assumptions about it now because the visibility is so poor.

Your primary goal at this point should be to stop *your* part in keeping the waters stirred. Ultimately, you can't make a good decision about whether or not the pond can be repaired, or what the repair work is even going to be, until you've given enough time for it to calm down.

By focusing on who *you* need to be in the relationship, retaining your positive behavior, there's only one person left keeping things stirred.

For reactive couples, because they're waiting for the partner to stop first, just you stopping what you're doing often stops the partner from continuing to do what he's doing.

## Maintaining Change

I mentioned in the foreword that *any new behavior, if it is going to become a habit or routine, needs to be consistently maintained for at least 3 months.*

Typically, what starts a person to work on change is discomfort with where they currently are – with themselves, with a relationship, or with life. So, *the initial motivation is based on negative feelings.* We feel so bad we've got to do something, anything, to make it better. So we start an exercise routine, or a diet, or saving money, or dinners out together. Once a decision has been made and a course of action taken, if it's a positive choice and relieves the initial discomfort, the good feelings it generates provides the momentum for continuing to do the work of change. So, the motivation becomes focused on the positive *over time* - but not usually at the start.

There are two typical mishaps that occur when changing a routine. The first mishap is that we'll think about starting the new routine, talk to others about it, and plan it in our heads – and then that relief we feel from having gone that far calms our initial distress and we don't take it any further. So the new routine never happens. Our discomfort gradually comes back until once more we start another plan.

Keep in mind that I referred to a *new* routine. The *old* routine is whatever your routine has been *without* the new routine. If the new routine is regular exercise, the old routine was *not* exercising. And "not exercising" meant all the idle activities you were engaged in instead of exercise. Because the lack of exercise was a routine of its own, it had its own momentum. To start exercising is stepping out of that old pattern, which we may have put a lot of time into creating. If the old pattern has existed for quite a while, it has a strength of its own. Just as if the situation were reversed and you had an established routine of exercising and you suddenly stopped - becoming *inactive* would be very uncomfortable.

The second mishap occurs when we are finally successful with actually implementing a new plan, get rolling pretty well, get some positives out of it and then get distracted little by little by other things and the routine starts to suffer until we've backslid again. In other words, the second mishap is with trouble maintaining motivation and focus once we've achieved our initial goal of starting a new routine.

The central point to all of this is that most of us are uncomfortable with discomfort. While we may go to great lengths to relieve our discomfort, often times, the discomfort is what motivates us to continue to do the work. It is important to recognize *that in order to maintain motivation, you need to be willing to hang on to a portion of the discomfort that got you started.*

If I don't allow myself to become complacent in my relationship, if I view it as a continual growth process and something that I can lose if I take it for granted, then I am more likely to maintain a degree of effort to keep the relationship fit and trim.

◆　◆　◆

How we typically try to motivate our partner to change is to usually raise *their* discomfort level by complaining. While this sometimes works, you have to be careful because there is the risk of creating an unhealthy pattern for the relationship. You're shaping each other to expect that nothing changes until you make your partner's life miserable. He doesn't like feeling miserable and you don't like having to push it to that degree. But the problem becomes if you don't continue to complain the behavior slips back to what it was. One partner is depending on the other to externally motivate them in a negative way.

At some point the partner has to internalize the need to provide his own motivation to be disciplined with change. Otherwise, what you've created is a Parent-Child dynamic.

I'll get into it more in Chapter 9, but for lasting relationship change, some form of accountability routine needs to be present.

◆　◆　◆

Another primary aspect to staying motivated is *awareness of the present moment*. As long as my focus is on starting a new routine next week, or somewhere in the future, chances are it doesn't ever reach the present day. "Tomorrow never comes."

I will often see couples who are trying to establish new routines in their relationship where weeks go by and they haven't even found time to do the homework I've given them for their counseling sessions. They seem to feel that there's never enough time because they allow their schedules and events to manage them, rather than the other way around. When we sat down and looked at it, there was certainly time for TV and other passive time-filler activities, but because these were things done "in the moment", rather than planned, it was more of an afterthought. When it was pointed out that that could have been time used to get the homework done, it was obvious in hindsight. If only there had been awareness in that moment when the TV was a choice, "Oh, this would be a good time to get our homework done", it could have happened.

Ultimately, we are taking a huge step towards living a conscious life when we teach ourselves to take advantage of immediate opportunities, to act in the moment, to be focused on **NOW**.

◆　◆　◆

What motivates some to do the work is remembering to balance the work with play.

If we view relationship change as work, for many people it's already being viewed as a negative. But if we are able to find ways of turning the work into play, we are turning a potential negative into a positive.

If, in trying to start an exercise routine, we choose physical activities that we really like, then we're already more motivated to take part. If we start to run, but we hate running, we've already sabotaged our progress.

If we try to think of how we can have more quality time with our partner by thinking of some really fun things we can do together, then I'm putting the "work" in a positive perspective. Breathing life back into a neglected romance should have its own built-in rewards.

◆　◆　◆

We need to remember to stay focused on the big picture. Hopefully, the end goal of what you are trying to accomplish is such a positive one that, if you keep in mind the end result, it fuels itself.

If I'm only focusing on how much work it is to learn how to communicate more accurately with my partner, then I'm working against myself because I'm only thinking about the immediate demanding effort. But if I keep thinking of how much this is going to improve the relationship and how great that will be, then I'm continuing to move forward in that positive direction.

For some people, creating a clear visual of what they are trying to work towards is helpful. Instead of putting a very unflattering picture of themselves on the refrigerator to make them uncomfortable enough to start exercising, some people will choose pictures from the past that were very flattering as incentive to get back to that. What successfully inspires one is different for another.

Many people overly focus on the negative of the present to the point that they become immobilized. For them, there has to be a future focus on the positive that is enough to lift them above where they're currently at. I don't mean this in a denial sense, that they're lying to themselves in order to get by. I'm referring to where that positive future goal is such an inspiration in the immediate moment that it moves them forward to becoming the person they know they should be, and closer to that future becoming a reality.

◆ ◆ ◆

In romantic relationships, ideally, you have two people working on improving things. When one starts to slip, the other is there to help support, inspire and cue the other onward.

Unfortunately, in many relationships, the health of the relationship is often placed on one person rather than the two sharing the responsibility. The one becomes the thermometer for the relationship, but it becomes a burden to maintain that role over time because he's not just representing his own needs, but also the health of "us".

Sometimes this happens because of the tendency to not duplicate roles in a relationship - if my partner handles the laundry, I'm not going to worry about it because I know it's being handled. So the unconscious thinking becomes, "If there's a problem with us, she'll let me know."

Typically whoever is the more relationship-based of the couple automatically takes on this responsibility, most likely the woman. But ultimately it's understanding that this is one role in the relationship that needs to always be shared - both looking out for the health of us.

◆ ◆ ◆

I did a summer group for emotionally-disturbed early adolescents many years ago. The group of professionals that was designing the program was well-intentioned and had put a lot of time into planning everything. We designed the program so that if a child misbehaved they would get a check on the board. Each check would deprive them of a group privilege and three checks would mean a loss of all privileges for that particular segment of the program for that day.

In the first thirty minutes of the class, 90 percent of the group had all three of their checks and had lost all of their privileges – which meant that they had nothing left to work towards for the remaining thirty minutes. It was chaos!

We, the adults, quickly re-grouped after the first week of this and knew we had to make some big changes. Actually, it ended up being just a small change. Instead of keeping track of the negative activity, we began to focus on those kids doing the "right" things and rewarding them as it happened. And the "problem" kids began to want to get in on the action too. The groups began to focus on rewarding the positive and it was an excellent motivator.

Now, I'm not saying that you or your partner is emotionally-disturbed, however, I am saying that, *even in the worst cases, the best motivator is recognizing and rewarding the positive.*

You may not be seeing a whole lot of positives at the start, so you may feel that there's not that much to "reward". But there are two things going on when you're shifting your focus back to the positive – you're shaping your partner's behavior by identifying for him the things you like and showing your appreciation for it, and you're also re-teaching yourself how to pay attention to what's still working, rather than over-focusing on what's not.

When you were dating, whether you realized it or not, you created positive behavior in each other as you rewarded the things you liked with your attention and your affection. So, too, if we are giving out praises and other "strokes" when our partner acts in pleasing ways, we are showing him that he can be successful again with us. This is especially important if the relationship has become so overly critical that at least one person is feeling that positive effort no longer makes a difference.

## Resistance to Change

While change and growth are necessary to a healthy relationship, sometimes things *don't* change and you've got to decide how you're going to handle that. Aside from the differences with preferences, which we often need to just learn to accept, what often matters the most is *what we attribute the lack of change to.*

Often, the assumption for lack of change becomes about *character* or *personality*. When I say character, I'm referring to the core of who that person is and what they're about in terms of integrity, selflessness, sensitivity, wisdom, and discipline. So the assumption that it's an issue of poor character is that if our partner was a better person, this wouldn't be happening. Yet, it's important to understand that there are several other options we need to consider before we make that potentially fatal leap.

When there is lack of change in a relationship, it can be due to:

- A lack of *education*. By that, I don't mean a lack of academic education. I mean a lack of accurate information about the particular issue at hand. If the partner had more knowledge about relationships or communication, more tools he could use, he would be making different choices.

- A problem of *skills*. More than education, I may have the necessary information, but if I haven't actually practiced it, it never becomes a skill. Anger management is a skill – it is something you learn, not something you're just born with. If you've never had somebody to visibly model those skills for you, it may be difficult to know where to begin.

- An underlying *physical problem*. Any number of medical issues lead to lack of energy, sex drive, agitation, depression and other symptoms. What is thought to be a relationship problem may actually be the result of an unrecognized medical issue.

- An underlying *mental health issue.* Chronic depression, anxiety, self-esteem issues, ADHD, bipolar and other disorders may be problems that started before the relationship, or developed alongside the relationship, but still not be the fault of the relationship. Not recognizing that this is what's actually casting a negative light on the relationship leads one to blame the wrong source.

- A problem with *distractions* or *priorities.* A person may sincerely desire to change, and even know how to go about doing it, but the continued demands and responsibilities in his life keep him off-balance enough that he remains inconsistent with maintaining change.

- A problem with *overly rigid role expectations.* Couples will often attempt to re-create the roles of husband and wife by what was modeled for them growing up, or attempt to use their childhood models as examples of what not to do. But there is still a tendency to attach too many "shoulds" to what they think a partner should or shouldn't be, to the degree that it is limiting the relationship because of the rigidity of the expectations.

- A problem with *motivation.* A partner may be *crisis-driven*, meaning the discomfort of a growing crisis motivates him to change, but when the crisis is temporarily averted, he drifts back to old behavior – until the next crisis. He is dependent on something outside of himself such as his partner, or a crisis, to continue to keep him motivated.

- A problem of *reactivity.* Each partner is chronically waiting on the other to do the right thing first, giving up their own control in the process.

- A problem of *forgiveness.* Sometimes we discover that our partner's problem *was* alterable because he *has* made the necessary changes to correct past behavior. However, even though we have the evidence that change has occurred, we continue to doubt the change, and may even undermine the success of the change. This usually occurs when the problem behavior has persisted over time, and we've learned that, while it may go away for a while, sooner or later, it comes back. But now our lack of forgiveness is part of what's standing in the way of things moving forward.

- A problem of *secondary gains*. A secondary gain is what people get out of continuing to argue that may not be all that obvious on the surface. There is a maybe-not-so-visible reward for continuing to fight. Sometimes the payoff is having the satisfaction of hurting someone else because you feel hurt. Sometimes continuing to fight means you don't have to acknowledge any fault in yourself. Sometimes refusing to resolve an issue means you don't have to accept the change that it would require of you.

- A problem of *trauma*. A partner has experienced a past trauma in his life that has damaged his security, significance, or ability to be in the moment. His history continues to keep him frozen and unable to progress in his current relationship, despite no longer being in that traumatic situation.

It is true that when the issue is one of character or personality, change is unlikely since that's who that person is - it goes beyond just the choices that he makes. It's his unhealthy perception of life and the people in it, and how he automatically relates, or doesn't relate, to it.

*Character flaws develop through recurring self-destructive acts, avoidance of taking personal responsibility, a refusal to deal with emotional pain, or chronically putting self first over other.* Often there is a lack of emotional discipline or maturity. Because there is enough repetition of unhealthy behavior, the negative behavior is no longer an overt act, but a part of who they've now become.

There is a difference between someone who has committed a single, isolated infidelity versus a series of infidelities - or someone who has committed an isolated crime versus maintaining a criminal lifestyle. This is not to say that one infidelity or crime is a minor thing, but it still leaves room for doubt that it's a problem of character. It may be a foolish, impulsive, in-the-moment choice.

If it's a character issue, often, there tends to be an underlying theme of manipulation that is present throughout all of their relationships, even if the only manipulation occurring is manipulation of the truth.

*Character also has to do with intention.* Does he do those hurtful things knowing full well what he's doing, or is it unintentional, as in a lack of education or skills?

Their problematic way of looking at life and people is so second-nature it is very difficult for them to stay on top of consistent change. The work of change requires them to re-build who they are from the ground up – the unhealthy thinking and beliefs that they have lived by. Obviously, the longer engaged in the destructive or self-absorbed lifestyle, the more ingrained it becomes.

Often, it is only at a point of true brokenness, or crisis, that they ever see the need for change. To stay motivated, *they need to be willing to remain in crisis*, rather than finding relief too quickly, which goes against the lifestyle that they've created of avoiding pain. In domestic violence cases you will often see the abuser repentant so long as he's in jeopardy of losing his partner, and then it's right back into old behavior. He might have actually been sincere in that moment of regret, but it's only truly meaningful if change lasts.

◆　◆　◆

So how do you get to know a person's true character?

- Time
- Patterns of behavior
- Success at dealing with and changing problem behaviors
- Consistency in keeping promises made
- "Practicing what they preach"
- How conflict is handled
- How sacrifices are managed

- The presence of honesty even when it's painful
- Doing the right thing even when no one's looking
- Consistency in integrity between the public and private faces one wears
- What comes out during times of crisis

Most of the material in this book is written assuming a desire on the part of the couple for the relationship to be successful and healthy, even though they may not yet have the skills or knowledge necessary to accomplish this. However, when it comes to problems of character, it is not uncommon to see an individual actively engaged in working *against* the health of the relationship. He can be so overly focused on doing whatever he wants, even though it may be destroying him in the process as well, that he is taking everyone down with him. When someone is actively caught up in this cycle, he leaves his partner little choice but to confront him on it and even resort to ultimatums. If serious change does not occur, there can be no future for the relationship. It becomes an issue of mental, emotional, and sometimes even physical, survival for the partner.

Likelihood of change depends on:

- a sincere willingness, and "readiness", to change
- the willingness to get professional help
- a commitment to exploring the causes of the problem despite the discomfort that self-examination brings
- a positive support system that he is accountable to
- making a specific plan for how change will be initiated
- actually implementing that plan
- maintaining the plan past the point that the new lifestyle replaces the old

Initial change *can* occur due to external pressure, such as the couple separating or some other form of crisis, but lasting change occurs only at the point that the motivation becomes internalized.

One big reason for this is expressed in the scenario where the alcoholic gives up alcohol because of a new love interest, but then a fight occurs. Because his partner momentarily stops being a positive motivator for him, the likelihood is that he will relapse because he temporarily lost his source of motivation.

If the change has occurred because the individual has come to understand the *need* for change, and has embraced it because that is who he chooses to be, the odds for success have just greatly improved because the motivation is now *internal* rather than *external*. He is his own motivator - he isn't depending on something outside of himself to maintain that change.

That doesn't mean that you should ignore accountability in the relationship if your partner is engaged in destructive behavior, while waiting for him to become self-motivated. You still need to be able to establish necessary limits. But your goal isn't simply compliance; it is to create a better understanding in your partner of how his behavior is impacting you, him, and the relationship.

◆　◆　◆

Resistance to change isn't necessarily due to any *one* of these factors; often there is some degree of overlap. A traumatized individual can also be lacking the necessary education and relationship skills. Unbalanced priorities can also be an issue of fluctuating motivation, etc.

At the point that character judgments are made in a relationship, more often than not, the only thing that *should* have been concluded was that the couple had exhausted what they knew to do on their own, and needed to get outside help.

Because we are so emotionally close to the situation we typically have lost any balanced perspective regarding the "why's". So, while it is important to try to understand our partner's motives, it's also important that we retain some doubt regarding our conclusions. What we should be especially trying to avoid is embracing the "worst-case scenarios" before we really have enough information to make those judgments.

## Summary Points:

1. Motivation to change and maintain that change comes from being willing to experience discomfort.

2. We are more likely to motivate change in our partners through recognition of the positive rather than over-focusing on the negative.

3. The underlying reasons for the problems a relationship experiences (lack of education, skills, physical problems, mental health issues, prioritizing, motivation, trauma, reactivity) are often incorrectly assumed to be about character or personality. The true underlying reasons help decide the appropriate interventions.

4. Problems of character are the greatest challenge to a relationship. Their existence is often assumed incorrectly, but, when they do exist, they are the most destructive to a relationship and the most resistant to change.

## Discussion Questions:

1. **Do you keep trying to solve problems in your relationship the same way, even though that way is not working for you?** What keeps you from trying something different?

2. **Do you tend to have an external locus of control or internal? What about your partner?** What makes you think that? How is it possible to shift an external focus to an internal one?

3. **How do you attempt to motivate each other in the relationship?** How do you try to inspire change? Does your partner have suggestions for you as to what would actually be more helpful or effective for him?

4. **What have been the difficulties in maintaining change in your relationship?** What specific things can be done to correct that?

5. **In the past, to what did you attribute the problems in your relationship?** (education, skills, motivation, distractions/priorities, rigid roles, reactivity, trauma, character.) After reading this chapter, has your assessment changed? Based on your current assessment, what solutions need to be explored?

# Chapter 8
# A Model for Change

I'd like to share a conceptual model that I use to assist clients who want to form a specific strategy for change. At the point that an individual issue has been identified within a relationship, this model is ideal in helping to break down the separate parts and map out a solution.

I've witnessed variations of this model in different incarnations throughout the years – the "Three-Headed Dragon" video presented by Chuck Brissette, cognitive-behavioral interventions, Ellis' rational-emotive therapy, and Barnes Boffey's book "Reinventing Yourself".

## The Three-Part Solution Model

The basic concept behind the model, as I'm going to be presenting it, is that for any problem there are potentially three different aspects, or layers, that need attention. That doesn't mean that *every* problem involves all three aspects. It just depends on how deep the problem goes.

The first aspect, and usually the easiest to address, is the *behavior.*

Using alcohol abuse as an example, the obvious problem behavior is the drinking. Many people will over-simplify the issue and think that the solution is just as simple - stop the behavior and you stop the problem. So the abuser stops drinking alcohol for a day, maybe a week, maybe more, but then something happens – boredom, stress, extra money to burn, friends who want to party – and they're back to drinking again.

Part of what distinguishes substance *abuse* from *misuse* has to do with the presence or absence of consequences. Misuse is using something for other than what it's intended, but *without* experiencing consequences for the misuse. Or, if consequences *are* experienced, then the misuse stops. In terms of drinking then, for someone at the point of misuse, it is often possible to stop after that first experience of a noticeable consequence. The cost, or potential cost, becomes real enough that the behavior is no longer attempted.

Abuse is a different creature since misuse continues even though we have knowledge of the cost to us or others. We continue to use *despite* consequences. It's the child who puts his hand on the stove burner and gets burnt, but then goes back and does it all over again. Something's not right about that. To intentionally do something again that we know has hurt us in the past is potentially self-destructive. It goes beyond a mistake and indicates an actual deeper problem may exist.

If we continue to engage in negative behaviors that are costing us, or those close to us, there is usually a deeper need that we're trying to meet by hanging on to them. If we remove a problem behavior, such as drinking, the need it was attempting to meet, no matter how unsuccessfully, is still going unmet.

Since our core needs are always legitimate, we can't just pretend that they don't exist. If the need for this particular drinker was drinking was his means to relieve or escape his stress, the unspoken message from his friends who tell him to stop is that he should be okay with stress. In reality, *he needs to replace the unhealthy behavior with positive ones that adequately meet the underlying need.*

The particular replacement behaviors that he chooses need to be a good fit for him, not just what works for somebody else. If he's decided on exercise as being an alternative, he needs to choose a type of exercise he actually enjoys or it won't be a meaningful replacement.

Also, he needs to come up with a number of different alternatives. If his only alternatives depend on other people being present, then he's "up a creek" if no friends can be found. Similarly, if all his options depend on good weather, he's going to be hard-put on bad weather days. The more workable options he has the better.

◆　◆　◆

Sometimes, however, even when we replace the negative behavior with positive ones, the problem still persists. Usually, this is because the problem goes deeper than just the behavior.

The second layer to the solution model is the *thinking*.

It is the thoughts that we tell ourselves (our self-talk) that create, nurture or maintain the problem. Whether it's denial that we've got a problem, minimizing the problem, or how we rationalize continuing to engage in the problem, our problematic way of thinking allows the problem to persist.

Problematic thinking usually starts with a truthful observation which progressively deteriorates into a distortion, emotional logic, or a conspiracy theory. "She's upset with me" leads to, "I hate it when she complains" which continues into, "She's always complaining," and on to, "Why can't she ever be happy?" concluding with "Whatever I do it's never going to be enough for her."

Staying with the alcohol issue, the logic path may start with just the initial observation of "I'm stressed", which leads to "I need a break", which continues into, "I deserve a drink". Understanding the thinking progression can often lead to other important pieces to the solution. In this instance, we just learned that, for this person, drinking is more than just his stress-reliever, it's also his personal reward. He feels entitled to it, or that he earned it. That's one way how he rationalizes his choice. So we need to step back to the positive behaviors and make sure that some of those positive choices he's come up with will also serve as credible rewards for him.

Part of the thinking solution is to first track the different logic trails he engages in that justify his decision to drink. And then he needs to come up with positive thoughts that will help redirect him back to making better choices.

If he's stressed, he's stressed. You don't want him to lie about it. And if he's been being responsible, he probably does get to the point of needing a break. So far he's still within the realm of reason. But it's when he makes the leap to "I deserve a drink" that his logic suffers. And that's where the replacement thinking needs to occur.

Instead of "I deserve a drink", the replacement thought would be "I deserve…" and fill it in with any of the positive behaviors that he's already identified that he also views as rewards.

Often, someone who struggles with substance issues will use his friends or sponsor to help re-direct his thinking for him because, in the moment, he's too close to the problem to be able to think it through for himself. The 12-step program slogans such as "one day at a time", or "first things first", are all thinking strategies that symbolize a deeper concept, and are designed to restore focus. However, by mapping things out like this with the solution model, actually writing these positive redirects down, even if he's alone he can still walk himself through the process of re-focusing.

If the problem doesn't go any deeper, and both unhealthy thoughts and behaviors are consistently managed and positively redirected, the situation starts to self-correct.

◆ ◆ ◆

If a problem *still* persists, despite sound behavioral and cognitive interventions, it's probably because it goes even deeper, to the third layer. The third aspect to the solution model is a combination of how we *feel* and maybe even what we've come to *believe*. The problem with each of these, and why they are the most stubborn aspects to deal with is that they can both be *beyond* reason.

The connection between feelings and beliefs is that one is a progression of the other. Unhealthy feelings can start out somewhat unformed, without any particular identifiable thoughts attached to them, but then develop into irrational beliefs if they go unchecked; if we continue to feed them.[8]

Let's use fear as an example. Fear is about the expectation of a negative event – whether it's an "it might" or "what if" or "I'm afraid that…". If I act as if my fear is true, that what I'm afraid of will actually happen, it has now become a belief for me. I'm no longer treating it as "it might". I'm now behaving like "it will".

With the thought progression I just used that started with "She's upset with me" (which was just an observation) and ended with "Whatever I do it's never going to be good enough for her", that last part was actually his underlying unhealthy belief (as well as an emotional distortion and a conspiracy theory). If he treats that belief like it's a truth, then there's no way he will be able to be happy in that relationship since, as far as he's concerned, nothing will ever be good enough for her. By taking it to that extreme, he's just destroyed his own motivation to continue to try.

*When someone feels conflicted, typically the conflict is between what they think versus what they feel* – two different parts of the brain. We may know that what we feel is unreasonable, yet still be unable to give up feeling it. We may logically know that our partner is faithful, yet still have difficulty shaking the irrational belief that he's cheating.

Going back to the example of the alcohol abuse, it may not matter that he's stopped his drinking and replaced his thinking if he hasn't addressed the underlying feelings or beliefs that are sabotaging his progress.

The most identifiable *feelings* he experiences that contribute to his drinking are probably stress, shame or guilt.

In terms of *beliefs*, sometimes with addictions there is a buried self-destructive fear or belief, such as "my failure is inevitable", or "I'm weak", "I'm never going to amount to anything", "it's only a matter of time before

---

[8]   So, too, beliefs can be conclusions from what we think, but for simplicity's sake I'm going to focus on the beliefs that form from emotion.

I screw up again". He may live in denial of it, he certainly doesn't want to believe it, but it can still be at the root of his issues - he's *afraid* that it's true. Maybe it was a negative message that was thrown at him when he was younger, via friends, siblings, or parents; or maybe it was just his own internal doubts and fears that he's harbored over the years.

In terms of "the chicken or the egg", maybe it was his initial negative behaviors that led to him feeling this way, or maybe it was the feelings that led to his behavior. But, at this point, the problem is that his underlying destructive feelings and beliefs continue to steer him to live in a way that only serves to feed and strengthen those fears and beliefs. Basically, his feelings are now dictating his choices.[9]

The difficulty with this level of a problem is that *you can't just replace a negative feeling with a better one.* I can't get up in the morning feeling lousy and just tell myself to be happy. I'm going to have to *do* something, or start *thinking* about something (telling myself something), that allows my emotions to shift.

When it comes to unhealthy, negative emotions and irrational beliefs, *you have to be willing to live in a way that challenges their truth.*

For the person who's afraid of heights and now chronically avoids bridges, escalators, and tall buildings, he has to start going somewhere high again. He wouldn't do something risky such as sky-diving and likely overly traumatize himself, but he might want to start with gradual approximations of situations that set off his anxiety, continuing to stretch past his comfort zone, weakening the fear and ultimately disproving the belief.

For the hypochondriac who is afraid of his body failing him, he could regularly go to the gym, putting his body to the test. He's proving to himself his own healthiness, rather than allowing rumination to make

---

9    Which also happens to be the definition for lack of emotional discipline, or "emotional immaturity". That's not to say that everyone who struggles with controlling his emotional logic is emotionally immature, which is a generalized issue. For many, where their emotional discipline is being tested can be limited to just a specific area.

him idle and the stress of his concerns to be reflected in his physical symptoms.

For the depressed individual, even though he doesn't feel like getting out of bed, he has to force himself to in order for the depression to start to lift. The longer he allows the depressed thoughts to dictate what he does, the more he feeds and strengthens the depression. It doesn't mean that it goes away immediately, because he may have fed that depression for a while and it will still take time to weaken and starve it, but at least now he knows what he needs to do to start getting better.

That's not to say that for the alcohol abuser he needs to regain confidence by going to bars and proving he doesn't have to have a drink. He needs to remain realistic about his limitations and personal triggers with alcohol. But now, he will also start to focus on other need-fulfilling positive activities, and ways of thinking, that can allow him to experience a greater degree and frequency of success.[10]

So the ideal positive feelings that he's trying to achieve are: peace, self-respect and confidence.

The ideal positive beliefs he's working at embracing are: "I *can* make good choices." "I can feel worthwhile if I treat myself so." "I'm just as capable of success as failure." (Though you don't want to create unrealistic positive beliefs such as "I will always succeed.")

◆ ◆ ◆

In terms of relationships, let's apply this to the emotionally disconnected couple. The feelings are a lack of passion or desire, a sense of distance, maybe boredom. Maybe there's a belief stirring around that "Our relationship was a mistake". The couple became overly-involved in the roles of the relationship – raising the kids, paying the bills, building

---

[10]   I want to be careful here to not over-simplify addictions. I recognize that there are different causalities to the disease and, for substance dependency issues in particular, there is also the physical dependency piece, not just the psychological dependency – which is why I specifically referred to abuse issues, not dependency.

the careers, getting the chores done - but the emotional intimacy, the connection, was neglected. As a result of the neglect, the positive feelings have faded and they now feel like room-mates. So the current problem is that those not-so-positive feelings that now exist are pushing the couple to continue to do things that widen the gulf, to make the disconnect even greater - such as no longer spending one-on-one time together, or attempting deeper conversations. The negative feelings are making negative choices.

The disconnected couple is waiting for the feelings to return, or waiting for their partner to create those feelings in them, rather than looking at what each can do themselves to restore those feelings. Often, this is because many people look at feelings as something that are either there or they're not. If the love is gone, it's gone. But that's not really true. If love was there before, often it can be restored.

The solution part of this model (the ideal behavior, thinking, feeling/beliefs) operates on the exact *opposite* dynamic as the problem part. With the problem part of the model, feelings dictate the choices. But with the solution part of the model, *the need-fulfilling actions and the healthy, rational thoughts are what guide the emotions.* The feelings are now in their proper place, and gradually we step back into being in control of ourselves again because we've regained emotional discipline.

For many, when you first start to implement the plan for change, you have to approach it in terms of "fake it to make it", because the negative feelings and beliefs will still be in the way, sabotaging your efforts. "Fake it to make it" (a 12-step program slogan) doesn't mean to lie to yourself or others. It means that, at the start, while you're trying to make those initial efforts to create this new identity, or restore an old one, *you have to step into the shoes of that successful identity before you're actually feeling it.* The desired feelings don't come first, they come *after*.

So for the disconnected couple, the "fake it to make it" leap is recognizing that if I want to re-kindle those feelings I first have to start *behaving* in a loving way again, doing those things that a connected couple does to maintain their connection, such as restoring a courtship. And at the same time with my thinking, I need to doubt my negative conclusions by embracing loving thoughts that challenge those negative fears and beliefs ("Maybe we *can* make this work.", "He does have his positive qualities.", "This *has* been a nice time together today.", "We can still show each other love."), allowing the room to actually experience something that is emotionally positive.

The more we *over-focus* on forcing the emotional piece, however, analyzing every encounter for a better emotional outcome in ourselves, the more we can short-circuit the process, since emotions occur naturally, not artificially. Our focus needs to be on the doing and the thinking, trusting that the feelings will follow without trying to force them - the same way that our body knows how to fall asleep. The more we try to force it to go to sleep, the more we're getting in the way of something that our body already naturally knows how to do.

◆ ◆ ◆

Are positive behaviors more important than positive thinking? Both have their place, but it usually depends on the particular person.

Because irrational beliefs are, by definition, beyond reason, trying to reason with them directly sometimes isn't as effective as simply doing something positive that breaks us out of that emotional spell.

Many times people will *over-think* a situation and talk themselves out of doing something healthy. They need to adopt the Nike slogan of, "Just do it" and not give themselves any more time to think, since "thinking" for them just means becoming emotionally overwhelmed.

At the same time, for many people who struggle with emotional issues, often there is an *absence* of rational thought. And even if rational thinking does occur it's usually *after* the problem behavior and not before.

Staying with the substance abuser, it can be a simple process of him *feeling* stressed so he goes for a drink. No thought required. He has that drink because *he never took the time to actually think about the consequences.* He may make many choices along the way from getting to his house to the store or the bar, but he isn't actually thinking about what he's doing, he's just following the path to making it happen. He never considers "What am I doing?", only the next step to acting on his emotional impulse. For him, the new strategy becomes introducing *more* opportunity for thought to occur.

The same for somebody with anger issues – he was angry, so he lashed out. It was all instinct, no time given to think it through. The majority of strategies for anger issues is to help the individual be more conscious of his choices in the moment, to create more time to intervene with rational re-routes, stepping beyond the moment to think about the big picture perspective and what those negative emotional choices will do, what consequences will occur if they're catered to.

◆ ◆ ◆

We naturally label negative feelings as being bad, but, in reality, negative feelings actually have a healthy component - it all depends on what we do with them.

Healthy anger occurs when we've been wronged. It gives us the courage to take action and say or do something about the injustice, so long as we do it in an appropriate way.

Healthy guilt exists to convict us and move us to take responsibility for something we should or shouldn't have done.

Healthy fear serves to make us think of potential consequences for our behavior, or to come up with a better plan for something we're concerned might happen in the future. In its most primitive form, fear is our survival instinct attempting to protect us. If our fear register *didn't* kick in when we were about to do something dangerous, we could seriously harm ourselves.

At the point fear becomes unhealthy, it:

1. grows so extreme it emotionally paralyzes us
2. makes us over-focus on the things beyond our control
3. keeps us from taking healthy action on the things within our control

4. keeps us from experiencing peace even though we've already assumed responsibility for the things in our control

What makes it hard to totally dismiss a fear, or an irrational belief, is because it usually has some small element of truth to it. For instance, there *is* always the possibility of failing at something. There *is* always the chance that our partners may not prove faithful. But *focused in a positive direction*, that discomfort hopefully inspires us to do our part to keep it from happening. Though we're aware of the potential to fall short, we continue to focus our energy on succeeding where we can. If we're aware our marriage isn't affair-proof, then we continue to take steps to keep it healthy.

In the same way that negative feelings have positives, positive feelings have negatives. With unhealthy love, we can get lost in doing things that make us feel good, but are killing us, or our relationship, in the process. For example, if we are tempted by an outside relationship, which feels good to us, we can start entertaining unhealthy beliefs ("She's my soul-mate."), which will make it incredibly difficult to re-direct ourselves because now we're magically viewing this outside relationship as "meant to be".

---

The end result of the solution-model process is having mapped out the *ideal alternative* – a specific plan for the solution that will replace the problem. Once you've worked out the plan, the focus is now on the ideal identity you're working towards, not remaining lost in over-obsessing on the problem identity.

That specific plan becomes your daily personal accountability system, your focus at the beginning of the day, your review at the end of the day - keeping the solution on a conscious, applicable level.[11]

## Summary Points:

---

[11] If you're interested in developing a specific plan using this model, go to Appendix B at the end of the book and refer to the 3-Part Solution Model Exercise. It leads you through the process of how to personalize this to your situation.

1. Most problems can be divided into three parts: the behavior that supports it, the thinking behind it, and the feelings and beliefs that feed it.

2. Problems that are resistant to change usually have an underlying legitimate need that is attempting to be met.

3. We can only change our feelings and unhealthy beliefs through what we choose to think and how we choose to act.

4. For emotional issues, feelings tend to dictate the choices. In contrast, emotional discipline means that actions and thoughts guide the feelings.

5. The most direct way to undo or weaken an unhealthy feeling or irrational belief is to choose to live in a way that challenges its truth.

## Discussion Questions:

1. **Do you struggle more with problem behaviors, thoughts, feelings or beliefs?** What strategies do you use for correcting your areas of weakness?

2. **Can you recognize an underlying need to whatever your particular issue may be?** What other positive ways can that underlying legitimate need be met?

3. **Is there anything you find yourself conflicted about with the relationship?** Are you able to separate out the rational voice from the emotional one?

4. **If you have any unhealthy fears, irrational beliefs, or conspiracy theories, what would "living in a way that challenges its truth" look like?**

# Chapter 9
# Healthy Routines

As mentioned in Chapter 7, one big problem with positive change is how do you maintain it over time? Or how do you hang on to the good thing that you've already got? Usually it comes down to looking at the routines in your relationship that either lull it to sleep, or keep it awake and thriving.

There are three important rituals, or routines, that every romantic relationship needs:

- a courting ritual
- an accountability ritual
- a forgiveness ritual

## The Courting Ritual

Most of us are somewhat familiar with what courting looks like during the dating stage of the relationship, even if we didn't do much of it. Part of the idea of courting is going out of our way to show our partners just how interested in them we are - often by showing them just how nice we can be. Yet, all too often, once the dating stage has passed, we tend to stop doing the things that initially drew us together, yet wonder why we're now drifting apart.

One of the first things to go in a marriage is a consistent dating routine. And when the couple does go out, they bring the kids, the relatives, or the friends. But the marriage has to continue, at times, to take center stage. If other relationships consistently come first (even the kids) the marriage will suffer.

Our ability to function as a team is what allows us to manage all of the other responsibilities. In viewing everything as energy, we only have so much to burn and every responsibility uses some of it up. Our "alone time" with our partner should be time to recharge our batteries, enabling us to handle all of the other things – but if that alone time has become just another responsibility and not something we look forward to, something has gone amiss.

Dating is supposed to be time out of the regular routine to let us live a little. You're not *adding* to your list of responsibilities; you're taking a *break* from your responsibilities together.

When communication starts to break down, time alone with each other often becomes avoided. While we are conserving energy by avoiding conflict, we've inadvertently managed to cut ourselves off from one of our most important resources – each other.

We need to continue to keep the romantic sparks alive if we wish to continue to experience passion in our relationships. We can't assume that just because we love each other the desire will always be there. It stays if we continue to nurture it and keep it alive. Just because we still have a sexual relationship with our partner does not mean that the romance is still alive. While courting *enhances* the sexual relationship, a good relationship consists of more than just the physical.

The reality of our modern world is that there are time demands from our jobs, children, and ourselves. We do not have limitless amounts of energy to lavish on each. But we did make our partner a priority at some point in the relationship that convinced him of our love, and it is only natural that, if that priority shifts or diminishes, his experience of our love towards him will also diminish.

◆　◆　◆

The courting relationship shouldn't be a one-sided experience. This isn't an opportunity for the woman or man to just sit back and expect the other to exert all the effort. It is a *shared* effort to continue to show each other in thoughtful ways that they are valued.

Our three core needs are significance, security and fun. A good romantic relationship provides for all three.[12] A loving partner lets you know that you're valued by giving you continued recognition for the efforts you put into the relationship (significance). He shows you his commitment through his continued efforts taking care of "us" (security). And, through the courting relationship, the two of you remember to still have your fun.

It isn't all about going out on dates. It's thoughtful calls during the day just to say hello, to express appreciation about something, or to say that you care. It's an unexpected card, something extra picked up at the store while you were out, or a backrub that didn't have to be requested. It's being creative and continuing to do nice things just because you know how it makes your partner feel.

It isn't having to do conscious acts every single day to the point that you're exhausting yourself. Often the best surprises are the unexpected ones. The flowers received every so often may have much more of an impact than flowers given every day.

Here are some suggestions for your dates:

- Don't always do the same thing – the same restaurant, the same type of food, the same types of movies, the same hang-outs.
- Take turns planning dates. One week, let her plan it. The next, let him. This way no one has the "burden" of having to do all of the planning.
- Explore doing some of the things you have talked about doing in the past but never got around to.

---

[12]　Though this doesn't mean that *all* of our needs are met by our partner, it's more like *portions* of each need.

- Take an evening class or a workshop together if you can – a shared learning experience.
- Read an interesting book together, taking time to stop and comment on any insights or reflections.
- Take time to talk about the future – where you'd like to be five years from now; what your dreams for the relationship are.
- Try to find new territory/experiences to discover together.

If the relationship has gotten to the point where neither cares for the play activities of the other, then put some energy into finding new ones. Chances are when you were dating you did things with your partner just because you wanted to be with him. It wasn't about whether you were doing something you enjoyed just as much as he did. Courting isn't all about just doing the things that *you* want to do. The focus should be on continuing to do things that bring you together, where each of you is continuing to stretch just a little.

It's all about attitude. If this is the person you say you love and want to spend the rest of your life with, why is finding time together such a chore? At what point in time did visible evidence of your affection stop being important? Usually, that shift is because we've become lazy when it comes to "us", and our feelings are telling us we don't have the energy.

If you don't have a lot of money to spend, find things that don't require money. Picnics, walks, sports, volunteer activities, church activities, local festivals – all of these can be either inexpensive or free.

Don't keep looking for reasons why you can't make it happen and figure out how it can.

If children are in the picture, don't allow their presence to prevent you from finding time for the two of you as husband and wife. You are still treating the kids as a priority by valuing the marriage relationship, because you're also modeling for them what a healthy balance looks like. Do you want them to eventually go into their own marriages thinking that a normal relationship is one in which the parents neglect each other?

For those with younger kids, often the dilemma for the parents is lack of resources. Family isn't close by, or they don't know other couples that they can tag team the kids with, or they don't know any good babysitters, etc. But the more in-balance our lives are, the more resources we have at our disposal – the more likely we are to have a peer group to rely on. Because the couple has over-focused inward with raising the kids, and possibly become more isolated, they have detached themselves from the potential resources outside of the family.

Realistically, the courtship will take some "hits" during the initial first year or two with having a child, or when starting a new career, or when job demands are increased – but the challenge remains as to how we continue to re-incorporate the intimacy needs *despite* these changing priorities.

Part of the reason for continuing to court is keeping an atmosphere of playfulness alive, since one of the gauges for how far a relationship has deteriorated is by how little laughter there is. Laughter allows us to keep our perspective. It allows us to not take each other, ourselves, or our lives, too seriously. When a couple is no longer able to laugh together, typically, perspective has been lost and the relationship is in trouble.

*One of the only "rules" for dates is that this is not time used to further discuss issues.* We need to draw safe boundaries around this time together, and not allow the problems from other areas to corrupt it. It's supposed to be an opportunity to continue to share positive experiences together that can continue to keep the relationship healthy and fit.

◆　◆　◆

While the dating ritual is a vital routine, it stops having a meaningful impact at the point that things become *too* routine. The over-familiarity of daily living together can deteriorate boundaries and we start to become invisible to each other. So, too, even though a couple will say that they still have date nights, if those times consist of a predictable repetition (dinner and a movie, dinner and a movie…), they start to lose the depth of what this healthy routine is meant to accomplish.

While we can keep the door to greater intimacy open by focusing on each other's "love language", it doesn't mean that we're actually walking through that door and going deeper. A continuing courtship is attempting to develop a more mature bond, a deeper intimacy, that goes beyond just having lived our lives together – and that requires a sharing that goes beyond the everyday experience of what we did in that day. It's going behind the scenes to that inner world where each of us lives, to where we make sense out of life and our experiences, to where we feel and think and wonder about life ahead and behind.

For some, it's helping a partner go to places that he hasn't been before. Some people aren't good with looking at themselves, their lives, or their motivations - why they are the way they are. They prefer to stay on the surface because going deeper is an unfamiliar place, and maybe a painful or scary one – you don't know what you're going to find if you haven't been there much in the past. For some, it's perceived as too much work. But our ability to go deeper (aside from being a help to the partner who doesn't know how to go deeper) is what allows us to connect more intimately, and makes us more interesting to each other. It affirms that there are more worlds to be explored together than just the one that's in front of our eyes.

So when I refer to quality time, it isn't just about the partner being present. That may be a step up from how things usually are, but just being present doesn't mean "interactive". Quality time in a dating routine is doing things that go beyond a passive activity that requires no meaningful dialogue. It's choosing activities that stir our thoughts or emotions, that create new dialogue, and may even bring facets of us to the surface that we don't normally get to see or explore.

## Accountability Rituals

When it comes to an accountability ritual or routine, this is how the couple monitors necessary change in a very conscious way, as well as provides necessary recognition for positive efforts made. This is one of the most important keys to maintaining change over time. The idea is that the more we approach our relationships on a very conscious level in terms of "what's working" and "what needs work" the less likely it is for blind spots to develop or for the relationship to subtly deteriorate, getting side-tracked once again.

Many times our tendency is to approach accountability with our partner only when things get to a point of complete discomfort. Or, rather than approaching each other with loving accountability, we allow things to build up until we explode and now the issue's out, but there's a lot of collateral damage to attend to. Having accountability routines in place, where both the positive and not-so-positive are recognized and addressed, creates a necessary platform where it's not about nagging, but keeping the relationship healthy.

There are three rituals I use to accomplish this:

- The Needs List Utility
- The Weekly Sit-down
- The Priority Assessment

## The Needs List Utility

An irony in many relationships is that a couple can become very upset by feeling that their needs are going unmet, when, in actuality, both sides may still be putting energy into pleasing each other. However, they often are trying to please each other in the way they *think* their partner wants to be pleased, or how *they themselves* want to be pleased, and are "missing the boat" as a result.

Keep in mind that what is important to you and your partner may change over the course of a relationship. Usually the first major "change" takes place in the first year of marriage, adjusting to the shift from dating to being married. After that, romantic relationships tend to reach critical points about every 5 to 7 years (if life circumstances don't make it sooner) just as your body goes through changes in cycles.

Life circumstances such as a move, change in jobs, or having children can bring about new adjustment periods since they automatically create new demands on the roles of husband and wife. What was important when you first started dating may now be inconsequential or even no longer desired (for example: you don't go out as much socially). And, vice versa, things that were overlooked during the courting period may now have become important as the relationship has become more serious (money becomes an issue). If you're not comparing notes every now and then to make sure you're keeping up with each other's changing surface needs, you may be putting energy into the wrong places and exhausting yourself despite good intentions.

It's important to recognize the difference between knowing what your partner wants from you and how he expects you to accomplish that. You may know that trust is very important to your partner. Trust is part of the security need. But do you know specifically what he looks for from you in order to develop that trust? Is it making the occasional phone call from work? Is it never going out to dinner with someone of the opposite sex? Just because you've voiced your needs in general terms does not mean you've gained an understanding of the specifics required to meet that need.

I have already talked about the difference between a need and a preference. You may *prefer* your mate to perform a particular sex act. You may even desire it so badly that you feel that it is a need. But your preference is for that specific act, the surface need is for sex or intimacy, while the core needs remain significance, security and fun. You *prefer* that he meet that need in a certain way, but he is not obligated to satisfy that desire if he has an aversion to that particular sex act because there are still other ways of satisfying the surface need.

This is part of the personal process of exploring our own needs in the relationship. It's why the first exercise I do in couples counseling is to have the couple complete a *needs list*.

A needs list serves several purposes.

- It gives a specific direction for meeting each other's needs.

- It helps clarify needs for those that really aren't in touch with their own needs.

- It can help establish a clear priority as to which surface needs are most important to each of you.

- It helps stop the "blame game" of over-focusing on each other's part, and gives you something within your own control to do for the health of the relationship.

- For those couples who are trying to figure out if there *is* a future for the relationship, it is a very simple tool to use to help arrive at a decision. If you are identifying something as a need, something you *have* to have in order to be content in the relationship, and your partner is saying that he is unwilling or unable to provide that, it helps simplify perspective in terms of whether or not the relationship can move forward.

Some people have difficulty with the idea of a needs list because they feel that it is putting the relationship in conditional terms. "I will continue to love you so long as you are doing this, this and this..." But I had spoken earlier in the book about trying to approach the expectations in a relationship as things you worked towards meeting for each other because of your *choice*, because you *love* each other, *not* because they were being demanded. The needs list isn't supposed to be about adding another "to do" list to all of those other lists already in existence. Neither is it supposed to be a complaint list for how each has fallen short. It is simply a direct and accurate guide to what is most important to each of you, and what are the best and most valued ways to show each other you are loved.

The needs list isn't just about what you need that you *aren't* getting, but also the things that you already are. It's a *balanced* exercise. Recognizing that, over time, we tend to focus on the things we need "fixed" and take for granted what is still working, it's just as important to sit back and take stock in those needs that are already being satisfied - giving credit where credit is due.

Recognizing creativity, the needs list isn't about micro-managing our partners' positive behavior towards us. It's helping to lead them to what works best for us, but it's still up to them how exactly they go about it. The idea of identifying several different avenues to meeting each other's needs allows for freedom of choice, in the same way that we might ask our kids, "Give me a top 5 of the things you might like for your birthday".

I'm mentioning the needs list in this chapter on routines because it is something that is directly plugged in to how you choose to go about courting each other, and the weekly sit-downs we are about to discuss. Also, it isn't a one-time exercise. Used wisely, a needs list undergoes refinement from time to time.

Most people's initial needs lists are relatively unrefined, especially for those that aren't in touch with many of their needs. As time goes by, hopefully, we are continuing to update and revise the list as we learn more about ourselves and what is most important to us at that particular point in time in our lives.[13]

## The Weekly Sit-down

Most couples who come for counseling typically have stock-piled issues to the point that things are becoming, if not already are, overwhelming. Whether it's because they have been unsuccessful in resolving issues, have too many other things going on that keep the issues unaddressed, or get side-tracked by bringing up other issues to the degree that nothing gets worked through, one of the most important routines you can introduce into your relationship is that of "the sit-down". This is a routine that can be used for:

- couples who have a habit of letting things go too long without discussing them
- couples who seem to never have the time to talk things through
- couples who need to practice their listening skills
- couples who are just learning how to use resolution tools
- couples who are practicing approaching and re-approaching in order to learn how to manage their anger without getting out of control
- couples who are trying to learn how to do regular maintenance on the relationship

---

[13]    To actually do a needs list, refer to Appendix B.

The couple initially schedules a time (at the beginning, once a week would be recommended) to sit down and review how the week has gone. If you can't find thirty minutes out of your week to do this, it's a good indicator that your priorities are out of balance. Usually this is on a Sunday afternoon or evening, since it's wrapping up the week behind and getting re-focused on the week ahead.

Part of meeting on a regular basis is to give some focused time for recognizing what's been working and what still needs work – the positives and the not-so-positive. Because there's time allowed for preparation, to think ahead about what your issues are, how best to express them, and what are some possible solutions, you've got a better chance of success. If you don't have time to address something during the week, you know that it can wait until the weekly sit-down to discuss it.

I am not suggesting that this meeting time be an excuse to delay talking about the things that require immediate attention. The sit-down time is a back-up system that acts as a net catching those things that managed to go unresolved during the week.

Another reason for such meetings is that they serve as a way of separating the problems from the rest of the relationship. In other words, couples can get to the point where most of their time spent together focuses on the problems. And so the relationship becomes one big problem because whenever you go anywhere you naturally get back into discussing what's wrong. It's important to learn to separate problems from those parts of the relationship that are still working.

For some people, if one little area of the relationship is out of joint, they will not allow themselves to enjoy the rest. This is often when you get into situations where withholding is occurring. One familiar scenario is where one partner withholds sex from the other because he hasn't agreed to her terms in some other area of the relationship. While she may feel that she cannot approach physical intimacy so long as he is ignoring her need elsewhere, it turns the sexual relationship into a control issue - which is a very dangerous thing.

I understand that there are factors that interfere with both men and women being able to participate in a physical relationship with their partner whether they want to or not. What I am saying is that *it's important to try to isolate and salvage those areas of the relationship that are still intact because these are what will keep the relationship afloat while the repair work is being done elsewhere.*

Sit-down time needs to be split between giving appropriate recognition for the successes, and refining solutions to the relationship problems as a *team*, not individual accusers of the other. Hopefully, the arrived-at solutions are balanced in that they involve what *both* sides can do to assist with the current issues.

The first time you do a sit-down session at home it may seem very awkward. Some folks don't know where to start, while others have extensive backlogs of things they want to talk about – though the typical length of a sit-down is about twenty to thirty minutes. It's not a marathon. Keeping it short helps keep the couple focused on what are the most important things to discuss. Each partner should feel that he gets equal time, and gets to address something important to him.

If a conversation is productive, you might want to go past the normal time frame. And sometimes it might be alright to focus on just one person's issues for that sit-down if the other partner is alright with that and doesn't have something they need to address as well. This isn't about creating an overly rigid structure. It needs to be something that the couple can adapt to their own particular style, so long as it actually works.

Ideally, the first sit-down should be done after you've completed your needs list. The needs list becomes the initial topic of discussion, where you're making sure each of you understands specifically what the other needs and how they are hoping for those needs to be met. This is an important opportunity to discuss the dilemmas that interfere with meeting those needs.

For example, she says, "I would like for you to talk to me more. I want you to tell me what you think about. I want to know about your hopes, your dreams. I want to feel more in-touch with what goes on inside of you."

He says, "Well, that's nice, but when I've tried to do that in the past I feel like you over-react. You get all upset that I'm going to quit my job or leave the marriage when you hear that I'm stressed."

If the couple is staying focused on arriving at *strategies*, these comments should have been very useful. If she wants this need to be met, she *does* need to be careful not to sabotage it. If she truly wants him to share, she has to be willing to hear what he has to say without reacting to or punishing him for it. On *his* side, he needs to continue to risk sharing for the sake of the relationship. The strategy remains simple – he continues to try to share, she works on receiving what he has to share without reacting to it. On to the next item!

Some of these conversations might just be replays and others may require the whole 4-step process for resolving an issue (identify, validate, explain, resolve) depending on the degree of the issue.

Sit-downs can sometimes be a little overwhelming at first because you are, in a way, attempting to combine the majority of guidelines that are contained in this book into one sitting. You are attempting to:

- stay focused on the issue at hand
- treat each person's side as information rather than something to react to
- remain focused on solutions rather than fault
- validate each other's opinions rather than dominate with your own
- manage your anger
- take turns talking and listening respectfully

You need to have realistic expectations that if you haven't had much success with resolution in the past, it's going to take practice before you see improvement - which is why it's usually best to start with the smaller issues and gradually address the more complicated ones after you have become more familiar with the routine.

◆　◆　◆

The general structure of a sit-down looks like this:

1. What's working:
    a. What I saw you do for me this past week that I really liked.
    b. What I did for you this past week that you may not have seen.
2. What we're still working on:
    a. The dangling issues of the week
    b. The ongoing issues (the needs list)

Whether a couple starts with "what's working", or ends with it, depends on the couple. Some people need to hear the positive first in order to hear the rest, while other couples like to end on a good note.

The "what's working" is the time for each person to give recognition for positive efforts. It's time to give credit where credit is due and to help shape what works best for each other. It helps a couple force themselves to pay attention to the continuing positives.

If you do things in sequence, "what I saw you do" gives the other partner the information they need to be able to list "what I did for you that you may not have seen".

Some people have difficulty at first with the "what I did for you" because they take it as bragging. It's not about bragging, it's about putting the current energy going into the relationship on a conscious level. We often do things for our partner that goes unseen and, as a result, doesn't get credit.

A secondary reason for the "what I did for you" is that it's a nice self-assessment. If we, ourselves, can't think of anything that we did for our partner this past week, it's a nice wake-up call that we need to be investing more energy - and our partner didn't even have to point it out.

The "what we're still working on" is much better phrasing than the "how you've failed me once again" that many people use. I challenge couples to start replacing judgmental words such as "good or bad", "right or wrong", "stupid", etc. with "what's working" and "what's not working" when they discuss issues in the relationship. You can debate all day about whose way is best, or which way is right, but talking in terms of does it or doesn't it work tends to avoid the competitive, judgmental conversations. It's not about does it work for you, or work for me; it's about does it work for us.

The "dangling issues" are the un-resolved issues from the current week, if there are any.

The "ongoing issues", as indicated, are about the needs list items. These are the bigger background projects for the couple and require updating over time, which is why they remain a continued focus for the relationship.

Usually couples will need to actually write down what solutions they commit to, so it doesn't depend on recall, and then they can follow up in future sit-downs with whether or not it got carried out as agreed on. Otherwise, it's back to opinions of "I thought we agreed to this", when that's not what was said.

Doing sit-downs isn't about passing blame. It's about sharing ownership for the continued work, giving recognition where recognition is due, and keeping the relationship on a conscious level in order to keep it fit and focused.[14]

Over time, couples will typically reduce the frequency of the sit-downs from weekly to every-other-week to monthly, depending on how much there is to discuss. As the couple gets better at fielding the issues in a timely manner and coming up with applied strategies, the sit-downs become more about just the shared recognition of the positive efforts made.

## Priority Assessment

While you're working towards a balanced relationship, it's also important that you're taking time to look *beyond* the relationship, in terms of a balanced life and how you're handling the individual priorities.

---

[14] For more specifics on the weekly sit-down, take a look at Appendix B at the end of the book.

There are different priorities in everyone's life: self, partner, children, relatives, friends, work, health and exercise, hobbies/interests, and your spiritual walk. No one priority should take our constant attention at the cost of everything else – rather the priorities are separate balls in the hands of a juggler. You're continuing to juggle each of these responsibilities and giving them their needed attention. If too much time is spent on any one, the majority of the other balls get dropped. Stress sets in. Chaos looms. Yes, the juggling act in itself can be stressful, but a juggler who has developed that skill, at some point, comes to see the act of juggling as second-nature.

Sometimes work will come first before having lunch with your partner. Sometimes the children will come before a trip to the gym. But overall you're trying to pay attention to where most of your energy goes, and what gets the least. The extreme ends are usually where we fall out of balance – over-focusing or under-focused.

Most people put the majority of their energy into two or three priorities and tend to neglect the rest. *In times of crises, how well you manage through any particular crisis is often determined by how balanced your priorities are.* Men tend to get more of their needs met through their work and hobbies, neglecting social supports. Women tend to get the majority of their needs met through their relationships and their families, often neglecting their health and developing personal interests (though these stereotypes are changing with our two-job family culture).

Some will end up placing an incredible demand on their partner for meeting their needs because they have neglected so many other areas of their lives, especially other social supports. While it is important to be working on meeting each other's needs, no relationship should have the burden of trying to meet *all* of one's needs. A balanced lifestyle, with balanced priorities, provides for this.

Keeping this in mind, another tool for personal accountability that you can use for the weekly sit-down is a priority assessment.[15] While it is designed for the individual, it can just as easily be a couple's activity. So the focus is how much are we, as a couple, in balance.

---

[15]    Again, see Appendix B.

The outcome of doing a priority assessment is, hopefully, a specific plan for how you're going to implement restoring a more healthy degree of balance in your life. Doing the assessment is also helpful for those folks who think things are already in balance. By actually mapping it out, sometimes they're surprised at what they find. They'd become so caught up in the schedules and routines that they'd lost sight of the big picture without even realizing it.

Since we are sometimes too close to our own lives to have perspective on the bigger picture, sometimes it's helpful to invite feedback from our partner on the accuracy of our personal assessment – they may have some good insights (and hopefully not see it as an opportunity to judge).

Aside from being another form of personal accountability, the consistency with doing this kind of exercise allows you to feel like you are managing the direction of your own life, rather than life dictating to you.

## Forgiveness Rituals

As children, we are often taught that, when you've wronged somebody you're supposed to approach the person you've wronged and apologize ("I'm sorry..."), and then they're supposed to say in return, "I forgive you." But it is a ritual that often doesn't transfer into the adult world.

As adults, just because someone has expressed that he's sorry, it doesn't mean that the person he's offended may be at a place of forgiveness yet. Sometimes true forgiveness takes time – it can't be forced. To say we've forgiven somebody before we're truly able to forgive creates a dilemma, since we've still got our anger or resentment to deal with.

I commented on the issue of forgiveness in Chapter 6 ("Resolving the Issue"), but it's relevant here that I mention the need for every couple that is experiencing resentment for past mistakes to have a conscious routine where they're making a visible gesture to their partner of "letting go". The ritual we're taught as a child starts with ownership ("You were right", or "I was wrong", or, "I shouldn't have done that," or "I'm sorry that hurt you."), before it moves on to forgiveness. As adults, though it doesn't have to be identical to that, ownership of a wrong always makes it easier to move on to forgiving.

Of course, there are details that make this difficult. Maybe the issue in question has yet to be resolved. Maybe the problem's continuing. Maybe the partner is unrepentant. But whatever the case, we are trying to create a mutual standard of forgiving just as we ourselves desire to be forgiven. To refuse to do so is choosing to anchor the relationship to the past rather than freeing ourselves to move forward, which allows resentment and bitterness to take root.

Part of the process of forgiveness sometimes requires a resolution in terms of "What I need from you in order to feel like I can move forward again." It's important to handle this sincerely and respectfully, rather than a manipulation for compliance. Sometimes a partner's sincere repentance is enough, but sometimes we need specific evidence of necessary change if we're going to be able to trust again.

How a couple chooses to approach a forgiveness routine for past hurts is up to them, but it needs to be something meaningful for the couple. It could be a spoken ritual ("I forgive you."). It could be a certain symbolic gesture (making a list of past wrongs and burning it together) or act of kindness (flowers, gifts, cards, etc.).

Ultimately, if you do a good job with the courtship and accountability routines, the less likely you will ever need to depend on the forgiveness ritual.

---

The keys behind staying disciplined with these routines are:

- maintaining your motivation (love for each other, respect for yourself)
- honoring that love is more than lip-service, that there should be evidence
- not taking your progress for granted or becoming too comfortable

- attaching a conscious priority to making them happen – scheduling and following through
- keeping an awareness of the present moment and opportunities to act
- not allowing yourself to become too distracted by other things
- *sharing* the commitment to see them through

Some people need the rigidity of a planned schedule if they are going to follow these routines, while others can be more flexible and creative and still accomplish the core of what I'm trying to get across here. As with everything else in this book, fit it to your own style – so long as that style actually works for both you and your partner. You're not going to be perfect in being consistent or getting great results each time in the same way that you can't force time with your partner to always be quality time. But what matters is you're continuing to try, you're continuing to make yourselves available to each other, and, with practice, you *will* get better at it.

The positives gained from staying with the routines – a consistent focus on meeting each other's needs; routinely working through issues without stockpiling them; having a thriving, exciting courtship; and keeping your priorities balanced - helps keep your focus over the long-run on what's important. They're just helpful ways of maintaining your relationship on a conscious level, keeping your conflicts to a minimum, and staying awake on your journey through life.

## Summary Points:

1)  Attaching a priority to the relationship means maintaining some necessary routines to keep your relationship healthy.

2)  Continuing to date past the marital line needs to be part of the routine if you want to keep the romance, and emotional intimacy, alive.

3)  Accurately understanding how we specifically look to each other to have our needs met is vital. It's also important to understand that,

as time goes by, the needs of the relationship change and we need to be flexible enough to change with them. The needs list is one such utility for updating and refining those specifics.

4) Keeping the routine of a weekly sit-down is incredibly helpful especially in situations where too many issues are going unresolved. It gives the couple necessary exposure and practice in addressing things, but is also a time for recognizing the positive, not just discussing the negative. The central focus of this time is on finding solutions, not dwelling on problems.

5) Aside from the relationship accountability that routines such as the sit-down provide, it's also important to consider our individual accountability by routinely exploring our lifestyle priorities and making specific plans as to what changes we need to make in order to restore or maintain balance.

6) We need to routinely forgive, to let go, of any past resentments towards our partners that may be holding us back.

## Discussion Questions:

1. **How often do you and your partner do things together, just the two of you?** Do you feel it's often enough that you stay connected? Are you able to focus on just having fun when you go out on a date, or do business and problems play a big part in the conversation? Do your dates provide variety, or have they fallen into a predictable routine? What do you look for in dating that helps you feel close and connected?

2. **Are setting dates the responsibility of just one of you, or do you share in initiating and making plans?** Do the two of you have things to look forward to at the end of the week? Is time alone together something that is still sought after, or has it lost its spark? If everything has become serious, how can you re-introduce fun into your relationship?

3. **Do both of you feel like you specifically know what your partner needs from you?** When was the last time you compared notes on this?

4. **Is there an accountability routine already in place for the two of you?** If not, how do the two of you approach what needs to change? And how do you monitor whether that change persists over time?

5. **How balanced are each of your priorities?** Are there any priorities that are going neglected? How do you measure what is and what is not in balance? Are you and your partner in agreement about the priorities that need work? What's the plan for restoring balance?

6. **Is there a forgiveness routine in the relationship?** How do you go about forgiving each other? Is there anything currently hanging over the relationship that needs to be forgiven? If so, what needs to happen in order for forgiveness to occur?

# Chapter 10
# True Relationship

When I do couple's work, the first four or five sessions are mostly relationship and communication education. And, at some point, I usually talk about "the 4 Stages of Relationship", which comes from Scott Peck's book, "The Different Drum". Consistently couples really respond to it because of how it summarizes what every couple has to move through if they're going to move past conflict to deeper intimacy, a true relationship.

Peck didn't talk in terms of true relationship; he referred to it as true *community*. His focus was on helping *groups* of people experience a closer, more inter-connected relationship - whether it was businesses, churches, whatever. I'm going to refer to it in terms of "relationship" because I'm talking about the individual couple, and it fits just as well.

As far as community, the Amish would be a good example. Everyone in an Amish community has a purpose, and everyone is interdependent on everyone else.

Veterans often experienced a sense of community with the men that they had to depend upon in their unit for their very survival. Police officers and firemen will often relate a sense of community to their fellow servicemen. Even gang members will sometimes relate that what attracted them to the gang was a sense of community; a sense of belonging.

Once you've experienced *true* community, that level of intimacy, it's hard to ever settle for less, because you know what it means to live life at that level, and how empty it can feel to live without it.

There are four stages to reaching true relationship:

1) Pseudo-relationship
2) Chaos
3) Emptying
4) True relationship

*Pseudo-relationships* are relationships that stay on the surface. It's what many of us experience at social functions. You laugh at the right place, say the right things, and generally don't rock the boat. As a result, while it feels good that we're getting along so well, it can still be a superficial relationship.

If we're going to go deeper, we must pass through the *chaos* stage. Chaos is where we begin to approach deeper honesty. We verbally start to recognize the differences between us, and voice our opinions about those differences. So we start to experience our first encounters with potential judgment and rejection. Some of those criticisms may be necessary and well-intended, but it's risking rocking the boat.

How people often attempt to deal with these identified differences during the chaos stage is to attempt to *convert* whoever they're in relationship with to adopt different behavior, which communicates, "My way is better than your way", or, "You should be more like me".

Peck had two options for moving out of chaos, but I'm going to add a third:

- Retreating back to pseudo-community
- Moving on to "emptying"
- Ordering the chaos

Many couples never move past the chaos stage. They go back and forth between pseudo-community and chaos. They may feel like things have gotten better, but it's only because they're no longer addressing the issues – the issues are still there, they're just being avoided by making the communication once again superficial. If they attempt to go deeper, the issues once again rise to the surface, chaos returns, and the couple retreats back to pseudo-relationship.

*Emptying*, the third stage, is actively working at *letting go* of our need to convert others to our way of thinking. It is working against judging, and trying to exercise grace, where we can agree to disagree.

Emptying isn't avoidance. For a relationship to go through the emptying stage means that the couple has actually let go of the issues that drove them apart. This usually involves either:

- intentional forgiveness
- not sweating the small stuff
- learning to agree to disagree
- staying focused on the greater purpose of being together

While Peck promoted emptying ourselves of *everything* that keeps us apart, what I promote is that emptying is usually focused on letting go of the *preferences;* the things we would desire our partner to change that are annoyances, but not deal-breakers.

The third option is *my* baby. Most of the work that I do with couples and conflict resolution is around *ordering the chaos*. I teach couples to respect certain rules and guidelines, such as are in this book, for working through issues in respectful ways that prevent chaos from setting in.

Typically, the things we are trying to "work through" are those issues that are *need-related*. I can't empty myself of a need, since I need it!

Resolving an issue by attaching an order, or structure, to the chaos (conflict resolution) isn't the same as emptying. You are able to let go because the problem was solved. If hard feelings remain attached, however, despite having resolved the issue, emptying would still be necessary. So, while we can sometimes take the back path to true community through resolving our issues, rather than just accepting the differences, in the long run, everyone still needs to know how to go through both processes.

*True relationship* is moving to that place where I'm able to accept the differences of my partner because there's a greater purpose that we are sharing in being together. How people define that "greater purpose" may vary, but the focus is on growing together, progressing.

◆　◆　◆

How many people fill that goal of a greater purpose is taking on the two most common goals for a marriage: raising a family and reaching retirement. However, *both* of these are problematic, since *neither of these goals is focused on the couple.*

In raising a family, our focus is on the kids, not the husband/wife relationship. So while they may accomplish the goal of raising the kids, when they hit the "empty nest" years they are forced to recognize just how neglected the "us" part of things was. There is this greater sense of loss because, "Who are we as a couple without the kids present?"

Similarly, in reaching retirement, the focus is on reaching a time goal, or a financial goal, or both. But now that we're here, and suddenly around each other all of the time, we realize that we really don't know each other any longer because we've each been so focused on getting here that we forgot about maintaining the connection.

So, more-so than family and retirement, the couple needs to work at maintaining a focus over the years on how they're going to continue to grow and thrive together as a couple.

Sometimes that mutual vision is about incorporating the individual visions you both bring to the relationship - trying to support and inspire your partner's dreams, while not forgetting about your own. Too often, we give up our dreams for our partner's, or for our children's. Too often, we lose direction because we allow life's demands to be the only voice that steers the ship. While there are going to be times when we need to shelve our own dreams temporarily, because other things have to take priority in that moment, hopefully, we don't let them set for too long or we risk allowing our own identity to grow vague, possibly becoming lost.

Because a couple in true relationship has such a clear idea of where they want to go (what "healthy" looks like), they are significantly less likely to get side-tracked by such things as affairs and out-of-balance priorities. Any behavior that doesn't fit that forward-focused picture is more easily spotted and expunged because it is so obviously inconsistent with the shared vision.

It's like an athlete who has set his performance goals and is actively carrying them out. His daily routine is so built around accomplishing those goals that to break that routine, do something in contradiction to it, would be very difficult because it was so against the current that he had created for himself. Such a choice would have to be a very conscious thing to make because it no longer fits his lifestyle.

And because that couple in true relationship now has those common goals that become part of their lifestyle, it's unlikely that they will drift from them. So the relationship remains a priority and continues to grow over time. And by the time the kids do move on, and retirement gets here, there is no major transition to go through because there is still a clear sense of "us", closer than ever.

## Summary Points:

1. There are four stages to reaching true relationship (pseudo-relationship, chaos, emptying/ordering and true relationship).

2. There are three paths out of chaos but only two take you deeper.

3. True relationship requires a common vision for the relationship's health that goes beyond the kids and retirement.

## Discussion Questions:

1. **Where are you currently at in the four stages?** If you're not in true relationship, what do you need to do to get there?

2. **Is there a common vision for just the relationship, and, if not, what would be a good one?**

# Afterword: Balance

There is a word that most teens learn in science class called "homeostasis". *Homeostasis* refers to your body's built-in tendency to always be seeking a state of balance within its various systems. The interesting thing about it is that the body is *never* in perfect balance. One system serves to excite, another serves to calm. One relays pleasure while another relays pain. There are all these natural checks and balance systems that are at different levels of operation, each responsive to another.

While describing our internal workings, homeostasis is also reflective of our outer world as well. We are in a constant state of seeking balance in our lives, finding a workable medium that allows us to move forward in the world, not hold us back.

When our lives are out of balance, when bad things happen, when we've been emotionally hurt by someone or have hurt someone we love, we experience emotional pain. How we attempt to deal with this emotional pain can decide whether we move forward in life, because we've restored balance, or become "stuck".

◆　◆　◆

There is an important parallel between physical pain and emotional pain.

Physical pain is a warning signal to the rest of the body that something is injured and needs tended to. While we may fear the actual experience of pain, *the fact that we are experiencing physical pain when we are injured is a healthy thing; it's our body's warning system functioning as it should.*

If you were experiencing physical pain, yet there was *no* injury, your body would be *mal-functioning*, giving false warnings, as with the situations where a limb has been removed yet the patient continues to feel ghost pains as if the limb were still attached. It would also be a mal-function if you *weren't* experiencing physical pain when you *should*, such as with conditions like leprosy where the nerves have died - the smallest of wounds can go untended, even becoming gangrenous, because there is no signal of pain drawing our attention to it.

So, too, *emotional pain usually exists as a healthy flag to call our attention to the fact that something isn't right.* In those instances, it is our mind operating as it should, directing us to the problem. If we understand that experiencing emotional pain is a *healthy* process that exists to help us identify what needs fixed, then it isn't something to be feared or run from.

Are there mis-cues regarding emotional pain, as there can be with physical pain? Sure. A chemical imbalance, such as can occur with clinical depression, can result in experiencing emotional pain even when there is no reason to be depressed. So, too, with character issues, when you'd *expect* a person to be experiencing emotional pain as a result of a destructive lifestyle yet there is an absence of emotional discomfort.

If we are not in the habit of self-assessing, sometimes it is difficult to isolate the cause of our emotional pain and know what needs healed. And if we are unversed in handling emotional pain, or had no models of how to deal with it, we may feel a complete lack of direction in how to actually go about working through it. But the first step, as with physical pain, is to *attend* to the pain (not ignore it or push it away), and attempt to identify what's causing it.

◆　◆　◆

Seeking balance in a relationship, handling the emotional *discomfort* that comes from having allowed it to have fallen out of balance, means:

- working at resolving conflicts as they occur rather than letting them build up
- working at keeping things in perspective by balancing the maintenance needs (job, chores, bills, kids) with the emotional intimacy needs (courtship and connection). In other words, balancing the work with the play
- working at not letting the relationship become too needy or too neglected
- working at keeping the communication healthy, where there is active listening and validation
- working at being consistently supportive, loving, caring for and respecting each other
- working at rewarding the positive, rather than punishing the negative
- working at balancing grace with loving accountability
- working at being solution-focused rather than problem-obsessed

Basically, maintaining balance in a relationship requires *effort* - which can be viewed as either another burdensome obligation or as the positive work that is necessary to keep the relationship alive and thriving. Ultimately, *if the relationship is tended to on a regular basis, the less effort it requires (and less emotional pain is experienced), because it doesn't stray that far off course.*

Because we've learned how to pay attention to emotional discomfort, and not to fear it or ignore it, we can use its information to honestly address necessary change in the relationship and within ourselves.

Since needs continue to change as time goes by, and there are always other responsibilities demanding our attention, adjustments are a continual part of life. At the point of best balance you should feel the least stressed and the most effective because you are using your energy in the most productive ways.

◆ ◆ ◆

I have attempted to write these chapters with a balanced perspective - presenting the extremes in the different scenarios, while, hopefully, capturing the desirable middle. No doubt there are exceptions to the guidelines laid out here, but, hopefully, you've approached the reading in terms of how it applies rather than how it doesn't.

For some, the idea that our happiness and the success of our relationships is partly our own responsibility creates anxiety. But it should also be a relief to know that there *are* things we can do to improve the quality of our existence, and to have the kind of quality relationships we desire with our partners.

# Appendix A

# The Tools

# The Conflict Model

**Reaction**
Instinct
Fight or Flight - Offensive/Defensive - Attack/Withdraw
Superficial/Staying on the Surface
Punish/Judge/Control (Parent) or Tantrum/Manipulate/Insult (Child)
Extremes
Talking from the Anger
Closed Statements
Assumptions & Judgments

**1. Healthy exits**

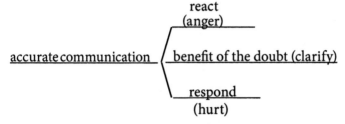

accurate communication

react
(anger)

benefit of the doubt (clarify)

respond
(hurt)

**Response**
Controlled reaction - Staying vulnerable
Working through it
Going Deeper
Reason/Explore (Adult)
Finding a Middle Ground
Talking from the Hurt
**2. Staying with Questions** – Exploration - Educate
**3. Benefit of the doubt**

---

**The Resolution Process**

Identify Issue > **4. Validate** > Explain/Process > Resolve
          listen                               **5. 2-part Solutions**
          acknowledge
          apologize
          ownership

# The ABC's of a Fair Fight

## Identifying the Issue:

1. **Choose your battles, and battlefield, wisely.** Pay attention to the time and place you choose to discuss an issue. And be sure that the issue is important enough that it requires discussion.

2. **Identify the intent of approaching a conversation to your partner; don't assume that he knows it.** Do you simply want a listening ear, to share your feelings, to get feedback, or are you wanting to resolve an issue? It helps to identify what you are looking for before you get into a conversation. That way you avoid guesswork on the other's part and you are more likely to get your need met.

3. **Confrontation is based on facts. Don't confront based on fears and doubts.** Fears and doubts are based on *possible* or *suspected* occurrences, not *known* occurrences. Confrontation only works if it is done in a loving manner, not a judgmental one. If you are tempted to confront based on your fears and doubts, then, what you probably need to do is seek information *first* in order to get your facts straight. What we often *truly* need is assurance – about love, trust, fidelity, etc.

4. **If necessary, attach a priority to the issue, so there is some sense of how important or unimportant it is.** When a lot of issues are being identified, it's important that there is some sense of scale to it all or the list will feel overwhelming. If needs are going to be met,

each partner needs to have some sense of which issues require a focused priority.

5. **Bringing up the negative past during an argument should be done only if the problem is continuing to occur.** Occasionally, there will be a past issue that has gone unresolved and felt to be a major contributor to the present mood of the relationship whether or not that situation has re-occurred. In situations like that, a re-approach is justified. However, in general, it is unfair to bring up the distant past since it distracts the focus from current issues, and is often used as a way to punish the partner.

## Validating the Issue:

6. **Balance the negative with the positive.** Just as it's easier to walk through a house and notice what needs to be done rather than what's already been done, it's important to stop and force ourselves to pay attention to what's still working. How can you positively motivate your partner to change only by complaining? When approaching your partner about an issue, try to think of a few positives to share first so he can see that you recognize there are good things happening too. If you are the first to identify the positive in your partner, it keeps him from feeling the need to defend himself.

7. **Own up to your contribution to the problem first, and it will open the door for the other to examine his part.** This isn't suggesting that you assign percentages to how much was you and how much was him. And it isn't suggesting you admit your part and then push him to admit his. If I can focus on my end of any dilemma and approach a solution, I am inviting the other to help me without ever "pointing the finger". We typically try to force our partners to admit to their part in a problem, but this often pushes them into a defensive stance.

8. **Take turns talking and listening.** While this seems elementary, it is incredibly common that the longer you have known somebody the easier it is to take shortcuts with your communication. And the

most common experience in mis-communication is, "You're not hearing what I'm saying".

9. **Be respectful of your partner's perception of an issue. Don't define reality for the other.** If your partner feels a certain way, you can't tell him that he doesn't feel that way. No matter how old the relationship, you need to operate from a position of giving the other the "benefit of the doubt". Each of us has our own perceptions of an experience but reality is somewhere in the middle. If you want the other to help you with a solution, you need to give credibility to what he says, even if you don't agree with it.

10. **Be willing to be wrong.** The wise partner is able to recognize that admission of wrong can be a faster path to resolution than many others. It's not just remaining vulnerable; it's about accepting ownership for your part in a problem. If you are staying focused on maintaining an honest relationship, and are trying to create a safe place for both you and your partner, admitting wrong is an act of trust.

11. **It's okay to disagree.** Some conflicts do not require resolution. It is unrealistic to expect that your partner must have the same opinions or agree with everything that you do. Don't make an issue out of every little thing that comes along.

## Processing the Issue:

12. **Keep in mind the goal of the conversation.** Is what you're about to say relevant to the current issue? Will it help clear or muddy the water? Is it to the benefit of the relationship or harmful? Discuss one issue at a time. Avoid counter-issues or becoming side-tracked.

13. **Exercise loving accountability while avoiding value judgments.** Try to separate the act from the individual – avoiding words that are a judgment of someone's character (lazy, jerk, slob, tightwad, etc.).

14. **Approach the conversation with options, not ultimatums.** Ultimatums are often inappropriately used as a form of control or manipulation. If you haven't already discussed options for possible solutions, go there first. Don't issue ultimatums unless you are prepared to act on them.

15. **Try to treat emotionally-weighted words as information rather than attacks.** In a conversation that contains sensitive personal content, try to focus on how this information can be used to gain better understanding. If the words are ones spoken in anger, try to move past your partner's surface communication and get at the underlying needs that have been threatened.

16. **Remain vulnerable.** It is more important to talk from our vulnerable pain than from our anger. Vulnerability is less likely to draw an attack since it is an act of kindness, not vengeance. If you are open to admitting your own shortcomings, it can encourage your partner to examine his, without becoming defensive.

17. **Don't negatively compare your partner to others.** Be careful of drawing comparisons too frequently, either positive or negative, between your partner and others. It indicates that you are using others as a gauge of your approval for your partner.

18. **"Never" and "always" need to be stricken from the couple's vocabulary.** There is no such thing as a behavior happening never or always. Using these words in an argument comes off as a blatant exaggeration and doesn't allow for those times when the negative behavior wasn't occurring, or when the positive was. It also puts the partner in a position of feeling like, "Why should I try?" if they are not getting any recognition for the times when they have tried.

19. **Make requests, not demands.** This is your partner, and you need to show respect if you want respect. Since you're not in charge of the relationship, it's not a good idea to assume that role with your partner by telling him what he "has" to do. If you want to keep things on the level of choice, be sure to term things as requests.

## Resolving the Issue:

20. **Some of the best solutions are the old ones – in seeking solutions don't try to re-invent the wheel.** We often discover that old strategies worked for the relationship in the past but we just stopped using them. Since they're not completely new ways of doing things, it will be easier to adapt them because there's already a certain familiarity.

21. **If you have already given some thought to possible solutions before you "come to the table" with the issue, it will move the process more quickly to a solution.** It's easy to bring up an issue in order to focus on how unfair or inappropriate an event or behavior was – a means of punishing. However, it's more helpful to approach an issue focusing on options. Don't go into the discussion with the solution, but, rather, possible solutions.

22. **Solutions should be tolerable to both sides, not a recurring imbalance of one side "giving in".** Try to avoid black-and-white solutions. A true compromise is the result of trying to find the middle ground where the needs of both are being addressed. Try to avoid two-dimensional thinking in attempting resolution since it operates in extremes (his way/her way, right/wrong, never/always) and usually implies a judgment.

23. **To forgive does not mean to forget.** To forgive someone for a wrong act means to accept (not agree or condone) what has occurred and move on, letting go of the emotional baggage that is attached. However, it is not advisable to forget an event since, "He who forgets the past is doomed to repeat it". Once an act has been forgiven, it is not appropriate to bring it up to assist an attack or re-create an issue. Forgiveness does not mean an absence of consequences. We forgive others in order to free ourselves from the consequences of un-forgiveness.

24. **Try to resolve issues as they occur.** However, each person should retain the right to put off an argument until he feels he can handle his part responsibly. The longer anger or resentment festers, the greater the damage to the relationship. If it is not possible to resolve an issue

before going to bed, then, at least, call a truce with a commitment to re-approach later. In order not to say something hurtful out of anger, it is better to give yourself time to calm down and think things through. Issues, however, should not be put off indefinitely.

25. **Decisions made from strong emotion are not going to be good decisions.** When you are having strong emotions your thinking is no longer clear. You may feel like you are still thinking, but it is your emotions that are guiding your thoughts, not your intellect. Feelings change from day to day. Reason is more stable and a better foundation from which to make clear decisions.

26. **Be sure "the solution" is clear to both sides and specific enough that it can be immediately applied.** People have a tendency to speak in general terms when reaching a solution; they don't define the specifics and so the exact expectations for each person are not often laid out. If a specific plan is made, it is much more likely that both sides will comply because the expectations have been clarified.

# The ABC's of a Fair Fight
# (Short Version)

**Raising an Issue:**

1. Choose your battles, and battlefield, wisely.
2. Identify the intent of approaching a conversation to your partner; don't assume that he knows it.
3. Confrontation is based on facts. Don't confront based on fears and doubts.
4. If necessary, attach a priority to the issue, so there is some sense of how important or unimportant it is.
5. Bringing up the negative past during an argument should only be done if the problem is continuing to occur.

**Validating the Issue:**

6. Balance the negative with the positive.
7. Own up to your contribution to the problem first, and it will open the door for the other to examine his part.
8. Take turns talking, listening, and be sure to validate.
9. Be respectful of your partner's perception of an issue. Don't define reality for the other.
10. Be willing to be wrong.
11. It's okay to disagree

## Processing the Issue:

12. Keep in mind the goal of the conversation.
13. Exercise loving accountability, avoiding value judgments.
14. Approach the conversation with options, not ultimatums.
15. Try to treat emotionally-weighted words as information rather than attacks.
16. Remain vulnerable.
17. Don't negatively compare your partner to others.
18. "Never" and "always" need to be stricken from the couple's vocabulary.
19. Make requests not demands.

## Resolving the Issue:

20. Some of the best solutions are the old ones – in seeking solutions, don't try to re-invent the wheel.
21. If you have already given some thought to possible solutions before you "come to the table" with the issue, it will move the process more quickly to a solution.
22. Solutions should be tolerable to both sides, not an imbalance of one side "giving in" most of the time.
23. To forgive does not mean to forget.
24. Try to resolve issues as they occur. However, each person should also retain the right to put off an argument until he feels he can handle his part responsibly.
25. Decisions made from strong emotion are not going to be good decisions.
26. Be sure "the solution" is clear to both sides and specific enough that it can be immediately applied.

# Appendix B

# The Exercises

# EXERCISE 1: The Listening Exercise

While the following exercise probably feels somewhat overly simple, and maybe even awkward to do, if you can re-introduce the overall concept into your conversations you should find that both sides feel more "heard" and, as a result, more willing to work things out. It's often immediately rewarding in that if you have had little success in the past with feeling heard, or your partner feeling heard, that it *is* within your ability to meet this need for each other. The education involved in this exercise is part of the process of re-learning each other's language. By breaking a conversation down into pieces, you learn to separate the emotion and avoid the tendency to react to what the other person says. You are learning to treat what each person says as information, removing some of the emotional baggage from your past history that you may ordinarily attach.

1) Pick a current issue or discussion topic for the relationship – hopefully something that is not overwhelming or has too much baggage attached. The conversation needs to stay focused on just one topic, without other issues being brought into it.

2) Whoever's issue it is starts out. If there are two sides to the issue, somebody needs to be picked to be the initiator. The initiator starts by voicing his perspective of the problem. He is not attempting to insult or judge his partner; he is simply focused on expressing his viewpoint of the situation - so his voice should remain calm and explanatory. Both sides need to have an attitude of patience in hearing each other out. The initiator is going to give his entire side, but he's only going to do it two or three sentences at a time.

3) The listener controls the amount of information that the initiator is giving. About every couple sentences she needs to stop the initiator to tell him what she hears him saying, before allowing him to go further. Rather than the listener *responding* to what she heard, or defending against what is being said, she simply *paraphrases* back to the initiator what she heard the initiator say. This *isn't* a word-for-word repeating, simply an attempt to summarize the content.

4) If the listener "got it right" by capturing the gist of what the initiator said, the initiator continues a step at a time until he's managed to express all that he wanted to say about that topic. (The reason for keeping it to two or three sentences is that if you say much more than that the listener won't be able to re-state it all because too much information is being given.)

If the listener got it "wrong", the process is repeated until she can accurately express to the initiator what the initiator is trying to say.

5) Once the initiator has finished stating his side, and the listener has finished paraphrasing, the listener should take a moment to find something that she can *validate* about what the initiator has said. (This does *not* mean that the listener has to agree with the initiator's opinion. It simply means that the listener tries to show simple respect for the initiator's viewpoint. It can be as simple as saying "I can understand, if that's how you were looking at it, why you would feel that way." Or maybe asking, "What could I do that would be validating for you with this topic?" finding something that the initiator can give the "thumbs up" on, that he feels both understood and validated for.)

6) It now becomes the *initiator's* turn to be the listener, restating what is being said to him - without reacting or responding with his own opinion. Again, the goal is to accurately reflect what is being said in the correct tone it is being said, and then, once the viewpoint has been stated completely, taking time to validate it, *before* going on to correcting any misunderstandings, or working towards solutions.

At this point, the new initiator can either go into her side of the issue if there is one, or simply respond to her partner's concerns – though still taking it a piece at a time. When she is done, and she gets validated, the sides flip again, back and forth, until the whole issue has been discussed.

That is the primary focus of this exercise: *attending, restating/clarifying,* and *validating.*

If a resolution is being sought, then the process can continue, moving on to discussing the suggested solutions, but taking turns doing so. If this is a 2-sided issue, then the couple will talk it through to a solution for each partner.

Note: If taking it this slow you still have problems with taking turns, give whoever's turn it is an object such as a small pillow or ball. So long as they hang on to the object, it's their turn. Once it's the other person's turn, the pillow or ball gets passed on to them.

# EXERCISE 2: The Three-Part Solution Model

1) Take two separate pieces of paper. Divide each sheet into three sections – behavior, thinking and beliefs/feelings. Choose a problem you're having either in your own life or with your relationship (your part of it). The first sheet represents you in the present. The second sheet represents the ideal, what you're working towards.

2) What are the *behaviors* that occur that either are the problem or resulting from the problem? For example, if the identified problem is getting angry, the behaviors that go along with that might be "I say cruel things to him", "I lecture him", or "I'll be mean to the kids" and "I withdraw". List them on the first sheet under the behavior section. Try to be as specific as possible.

What are the specific *thoughts* you have that are either creating the issue or contributing to the issue? Usually, the first thought in the chain is more of an observation – not much is being read into that first incident that sets off the train of thought. For instance, "He didn't take out the garbage again" is just an observation. But it may then lead to, "Once again he didn't do what he said", which might lead to, "It really bothers me that I can't count on him", which might lead to "If he cared about me, he wouldn't be doing this." Write the whole train of thought that goes along with the problem on the first page under the thinking section. Feel free to track as many trains as are connected to the particular problem.

What *beliefs or feelings* continue to occur that are complicating things? Continuing with the example just given, the feelings might be: anxious, depressed, sad, lonely, unloved, disrespected, betrayed, angry, disappointed, neglected, etc. The beliefs may be, "He doesn't care about me," "I can't count on him". Our beliefs can be conclusions based on how we feel, or our feelings can be based on what we're choosing to believe. It can go either way. Write down whatever your feelings or beliefs are that are related to, or driving, the problem.

3) The second page represents the ideal. It's what you're aiming towards; what the desired situation would be. Before you start with the categories,

see if you can identify the need or needs that you've been trying to meet for yourself by doing what you've been doing - even if it hasn't worked.

Then start with the behavior category, write down the positive *behaviors* that you need to be doing to replace the current negative ones you're engaged in. In this instance, it might be, "Try to educate him in a non-lecture way that this isn't about the trash; it's about him keeping his word.", "Letting him know I feel like I'm unimportant to him, rather than attacking him (talking from the hurt and not the anger)", "Let the minor things go", "Controlling my temper". Try to think of as many positive alternative behaviors as you can. The more options you have the better. Once you're done, look at whether these behaviors would successfully satisfy the need you've identified, even if just in part. If they're still not satisfying the need, see if you can come up with better behavioral options that would.

Go on to the thought section, second page. What *thoughts* would effectively counter the problem thinking? For instance, "The garbage being taken out when I want it to is my preference, not a need – not worth getting that upset about," "He does show me in other ways that he cares". The counter positive thoughts you're coming up with need to be thoughts you can embrace because they are credible and have weight. Don't list thoughts that you really can't buy into. They need to be ideas that, when you consider them, effectively de-escalate where your feelings would take you.

Lastly, list the feelings and beliefs that would be desired. In this instance, "I want to feel valued", "I want to feel like I have some control over what gets done", "I want to feel like everything doesn't depend on me."

The beliefs: "He *does* care about me, he just doesn't always show it the way that I want him to." "He does care about me, I just sometimes fail to see it when he does." "I can count on him, but I need to be realistic about what he can do." "I *can* count on him with many things, but I need to be respectful in bringing those things to his attention, and can't expect him to do everything perfectly." Initially, those beliefs you are trying to create may seem far from where you are, but the more you actively work on the behaviors and thoughts that created the negative beliefs, the more power you'll be putting into creating the desired positive beliefs. Obviously, her husband has some degree of responsibility in helping support the desired beliefs, especially those concerning him, but the important part is that the wife's focusing on what she can do in order to manage her reactions.

4) Having completed the pages, I usually suggest getting rid of the first one. It served as the template for establishing what you're working towards, but your focus now needs to be on the ideal you're trying to create. The second chart becomes your gauge at the end of each day as to how well you've progressed towards making that picture a reality. And it serves as a reminder of the things you can do and think about when you're being tempted to backslide or are feeling distant from remembering your alternatives.

---

The model can be used with individual problems or problems of the relationship. If you do the exercise as a couple, you'd need a set for each person's part of the problem.

Often, the easiest sections to fill out are the ones that that person is the most "in touch" with about themselves. The parts that are hardest to fill in are usually that person's particular blind spot.

# EXERCISE 3: The Needs List

The Needs List is a list of both his/her needs, NOT desires. These are the things that you feel are *vital* to maintaining a long-term relationship.

1.  Each fills out his own list without sharing them just yet. The list should consist of *both* the needs that are currently not being met as well as those that are. If you can't come up with some specific needs on your own, think in terms of the three core needs - security (trust and control), significance (valued and respected) and fun (quality and freedom) - and list specifically how you look for your partner to meet each one. Try to be detailed rather than vague. "I need to feel loved" is way too vague. How *specifically* do you look to feel loved by your partner? The more specific you can be, the easier it's going to be for your partner to have a clear idea of what you're looking for.

2.  Prioritize the list. Assign a value to the top three or four items that are the most important to you - but also need the most work. (This gives the partner an indication of the best places to start, and where their energy and attention will have the most immediate impact.)

3.  *Prior* to showing each other your lists, take the time to *guess* each other's lists. This is NOT an opportunity to punish each other for getting it wrong. This is about seeing how closely you understand what's important to each other or how far things have drifted.

4.  Go ahead and actually share the lists with each other. This is an opportunity to look at the lists and have your partner define anything that seems vague to you. Each person needs to have a clear understanding of what is being requested in order to effectively address that need.

5.  Turn your lists over to each other. At this point, the "list" is out of each other's control. Your responsibility is to work on the list your partner has given you, NOT on keeping track of how well your partner is doing in managing YOUR list. The focus is back on what is in your own control to do for the relationship to prosper. *Both of*

you are making a commitment to respect and work on each other's needs.

If needs are listed that either feels they can't meet for the other, now is the time to discuss them. If you are saying you have to have something and hearing a "No", you have come to a roadblock. If it is a, "No, I can't *yet*," or, "I'm working toward that but I'm not there yet," then there's room to work. If it's a "No. Not now. Not ever," then the relationship has reached a potential "deal-breaker".

The needs list isn't written in stone. If you think of better ways to meet those needs as time goes by, feel free to revise your list.

## EXERCISE 4: The Weekly Sit-down

What it comes down to:

1. **What's working?**
   - What I saw you do this past week that I liked.
   - What I did for you this past week that you may not have seen.

2. **What are we still working on?**
   - Dangling issues from the past week
   - Ongoing projects (needs list)

---

The Weekly Sit-down should occur, you guessed it, on a weekly basis. Aside from being a time to address lingering issues, it's an opportunity to give needed recognition for the work that's being done, positive feedback for the successes, and fine-tuning the works-in-progress. It also:

a) gives you continuing practice with your resolution skills
b) helps act as an ongoing barometer for the relationship (with feedback being provided in a neutral but supportive way)
c) helps you prioritize issues
d) helps you think things through in terms of what the issue actually is, how to best present it, and what are some possible solutions
e) shows your partner your willingness to work on things by participating in the process

## Guidelines:

1. Keep a list during the week of any issues, concerns or other items that you want to bring to the sit-down. They can be small or large, the goal is to capture the things that you might otherwise be forgetting or avoiding.

2. You can start either by addressing what's already working, or going to the list. It depends on what works best for the two of you. Just be sure to cover both.

3. For the first couple of sit-downs it's recommended that you initially pick some of the "milder" issues for better chances of initial success. Once you "get the hang of it" you can start approaching the bigger ones.

4. When you review the list both sides should attach a priority to the ones that are most important to be discussed. If you can't agree on a proper priority, just be sure to review at least one item important to each of you.

5. The atmosphere and focus should be one of sharing, providing information and seeking solutions – not an opportunity to attack.

6. Don't expect to cover everything on the list in one sitting. Don't turn it into a marathon. Allow for about 15-30 minutes to discuss things. If you have more time, fine, but don't force it. What you don't get to this week can be postponed until next week (or sooner, depending on the immediacy).

7. Don't expect to get everything "right" the first time. The idea is to practice hearing each other out, validating each other as you go, taking the time to really listen, and then to move on to solutions - if a solution is being requested. Success isn't measured by how many items on the list you resolve, but more-so that you've successfully taken the time to stay with the routine of the sit-down and made the effort at discussing issues.

8. Keep in mind that people tend to stop short or go too far. If you're giving up after the first ten minutes, you aren't being patient enough and definitely aren't treating things as information. If you've reached a workable solution, don't over-discuss it.

9.  Remember to keep things balanced by discussing BOTH parts of each issue – what BOTH of you are contributing to the issue at hand, as well as what BOTH of you can contribute to the solution.

10. If you find yourself getting side-tracked, stop every minute or so and check to see if you're still discussing the agreed on topic from the list. If you're bringing up other topics that aren't on the list, decide if they warrant discussion time of their own and add them to the list if necessary, but stay with the issue at hand.

11. Stick with the resolution tools (the ABC's) – stay focused, don't bring up the past unless it's still playing a part in the present, identify what it is you need, avoid making judgments, be willing to be vulnerable and willing to be wrong, try to find solutions that are win/win for both that may also require just a bit of stretching too.

12. Find your points of agreement, remembering to validate, moving towards solutions, rather than being problem-obsessed.

Just remember, practice develops competency. And competency develops confidence at being able to make the relationship work.

# EXERCISE 5: The Priority Assessment

1. Take a sheet of paper and write down the different types of priorities in your life: friends and family (social), health (exercise and diet), kids, spouse/partner (courting), job, interests/hobbies/fun (you), and spiritual (purpose/meaning in life).

2. Now take a few minutes and think of where the majority of your time and attention is going. For the priorities that are getting the most attention, draw a larger circle around them. For the areas that are the most neglected, draw a smaller circle. This is an easy visual to show where your energy needs to be going. You may need to be subtracting time and effort from the larger circles and diverting them to the smaller ones.

3. Take some time to itemize the things you do for each particular category. By itemizing, you may find that it wasn't as much as you thought, or maybe it was more than you thought. If you want to get serious about it, you can even itemize the frequency of those activities or the amount of time that goes into each on a normal week. (If you're open to it, invite your partner's opinions as to the accuracy of your assessment.)

4. Now take a second sheet of paper, which will represent "your life in balance". Write down the same categories, but now itemize the things you could realistically start doing in the neglected areas that would restore some balance to the picture.

5. Now that you've identified what you could be doing, you need to make a specific plan for how you're actually going to *start* doing those things in order for it to become a reality. That plan needs to start with the first simple steps that would lead into accomplishing the greater task. For instance, if one of the things you'd listed was to take an evening class, the first few steps might be to order a class listing, decide what evenings you have to work with, and decide from that listing what class you were interested in that fit with your available evening. The steps need to be small enough, and immediate enough, that you can start acting on them within that week. Depending on how easily distracted you are, you might want to continue to review the priority list on a weekly or monthly basis to measure your progress and keep yourself on track.

If you *don't* have a specific plan, it probably will not happen; you'll just know that it *should* happen. The priority assessment serves as your own personal accountability system. It's what you focus on at the start of the day to incorporate into your day, and what you review at the end of the day for how you did, and what you can do better at tomorrow.

In addition to doing this as individuals, you can also do a priority assessment for the relationship, looking jointly at how the time is being spent, and where changes need to occur. This can be delicate territory since it requires a good deal of respect shown for each person. It's very easy to slip into the miscommunications of, "My time is more important than your time", or "How you spend your time is a waste of time".

CPSIA information can be obtained
at www.ICGtesting.com
Printed in the USA
FFOW02n0939110615
14178FF